*"[The 333SP] was a simple car. The carbon monocoque was very basic, both shape and lay-up type. Everyone in Dallara, including Mr. Dallara of course, have very good remembrance of this car. We loved this car."*

**Luca Pignacca**

*"IMSA races were more than just racing. The spirit and the professionalism, the aim to give the spectators a good show, the fascination of the fans, and the high level of sportsmanship impressed me a lot".*

**Fredy Lienhard**

*"I think we built a total of twenty-six MK IIIs. My dad said the car hit all the marks right off. It was the right car for the market for the right price and a car that team owners knew was competitive. Without an engine it cost $245,000—a very good deal."*

**Bill Riley**

*"When the prize money started not being paid by Andy Evans during the 1997 season, I got really annoyed."*

**Michael Gue**

JOEST
PORSCHE
J. WINTER
M. SIGALA
B. SCHNEIDER
O. LARRAURI

# IMSA 1990–1999

## THE TURBULENT YEARS OF AMERICAN SPORTS CAR RACING

MARK RAFFAUF

MARTIN RAFFAUF, GEORGE SILBERMANN, AND JONATHAN INGRAM

OCTANE PRESS

Octane Press, Edition 1.0, February 2025


On the cover: The classic 1996 duel at Daytona in the morning fog. *Brian Cleary*

On the front endpapers: Parker Johnstone and Comtech's Acura V6-powered Spice-dominated Camel Lights for three seasons. *Peter Gloede*

On the back endpapers: Early action at Sebring. *Rick Dole*

On the frontispiece: The Porsche 962 remained competitive and won races in Camel GTP over the span of ten seasons. *Peter Gloede*

On the title page: Sunrise over Daytona Beach and still a long way to go in the Rolex 24. *Brian Cleary*

On the dedication page: IMSA tube-frame GT cars generated fierce competition for an entire decade. *Brian Cleary*

On the contents page: The walls amplified the high-pitched roar of Tom Walkinshaw Racing's V12 Castrol Jaguar on the high banks. *Brian Cleary*

On the foreword page: James Weaver was the lead driver for Dyson Racing in Porsche 962s and Riley & Scott MK IIIs throughout the 1990s. *Rick Dole*

On the preface page: Gianpiero Moretti putting the power down in the magnificent MOMO Ferrari 333SP. *Bill Tuttle*

On the introduction page: Jim Matthews's JMR Ferrari 333SP on the downshift into Turn One at Daytona. *Rick Dole*

On the back cover: WSC and GT cars always raced together at the longer duration events but often separately in shorter distance races due to too many cars! *Brian Cleary*



ISBN: 978-1-64234-050-1

LCCN: 2022943048

Designed by Tom Heffron
Project edited by Faith Garcia
Copyedited by Faith Garcia
Proofread by Tracy Bueno

**octanepress.com**

Octane Press is based in Austin, Texas

Printed in China

# DEDICATION

For all the participants, manufacturers, industry partners, event promoters, and fans whose passion and dedication to sports car racing propelled IMSA world-class competition through a challenging decade and into the twenty-first century.

DAYTONA · USA
JAGUAR
Castrol
60
Castrol
JAGUAR

# CONTENTS

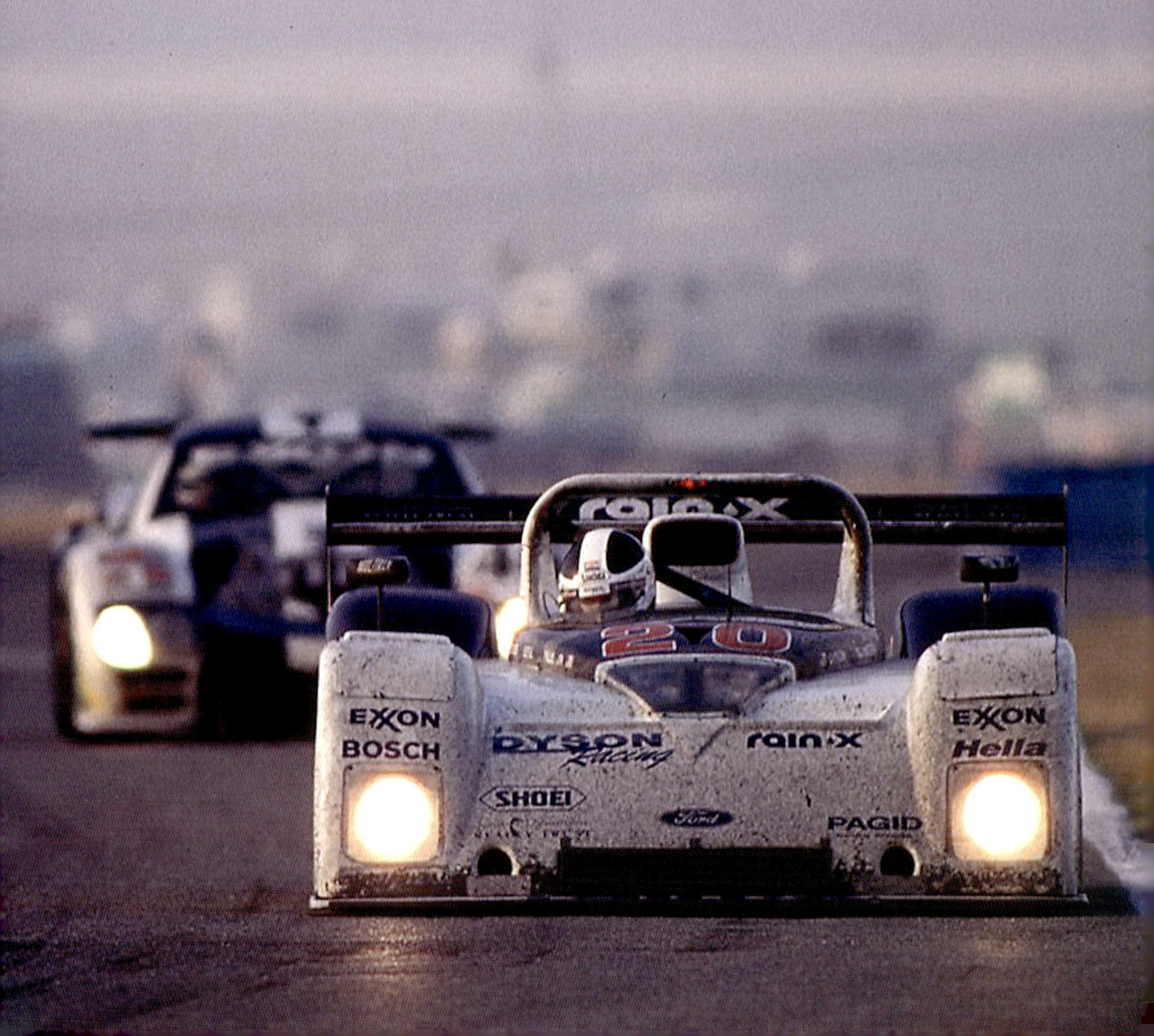
rain-X
20
EXXON
BOSCH
DYSON Racing
rain-X
EXXON
Hella
SHOEI
Ford
PAGID

# FOREWORD

By Rob Dyson

As an IMSA entrant and driver, I was fortunate to be present for some truly significant moments in the history of the series over the course of three decades.

When our team moved up from club racing and into IMSA in 1983, the organization was establishing itself as the top tier of sports car and endurance racing in North America under John Bishop's leadership, if not the world. The greatest drivers and marques in sports car racing were competing there, and it was where I wanted us to be. Within two years, we were well and truly "on the map," winning in GTP and competing for championships with Porsche.

During our time competing in IMSA-sanctioned events, the organization both boomed and experienced more than its fair share of roller-coaster moments.

When Bishop and the original shareholders decided to sell the series in 1989, it signaled the end of an era, and the next quarter century was both exciting and tumultuous. Through a procession of ownership and differing "visions" of what the sport should be, we were in the middle of it.

As I'm sure you'll learn in the pages to follow, the sport was sustained by the passionate commitment of entrants like myself, manufacturers, and promoters who prioritized sports car racing. This core defined IMSA racing. Whether it was the boom-bust years of GTP, the uneven World Sports Car era, the contentious Professional SportsCar Racing years, or the relatively restorative American Le Mans Series era that followed, IMSA-sanctioned events remained the bedrock of endurance racing in this country and in the world's eyes.

After 1989, the succession of ownership groups and "visions" at the top levels of the sport was frankly dizzying. Any fan (or entrant!) during this time who could keep track of series' names, class structures, and technical regulations could probably earn an advanced degree in international relations. The leadership's attempts to rein in costs vied with the need to appeal to manufacturers, and this bred a tapestry of attempts to wed the two, often with mixed results. But the essence of sports car racing survived: the fastest sports cars, driven by world-class drivers, fought for titles and race wins that were historically significant, no matter the nomenclature.

The fact that sports car racing could support multiple platforms in North America during its most strained periods was a testament to the power and draw of the venues and the wider desire to win the most storied events every year. Our team was fortunate to compete in all the sanctioned events and win races and championships in every single championship, whether it was the USRRC Can-Am or the original incarnation of the Grand American Rolex Series. We were blessed to have extraordinary talents within our organization and truly phenomenal drivers whose records sit comfortably among the all-time greats of the sport.

I'd like to think that we contributed a lot to the sport in our three decades competing at its top level. My deep love for endurance racing drove our commitment, and this passion runs very deep in our family. I'm proud of my son Chris, who attended the GTP races with me and was just a little boy when we started, and who became a two-time IMSA driving champion. Time flew by, and not a day goes by that I'm not thankful for the opportunities we have had and for what we accomplished. What a privilege it was to witness and experience this incredible era of racing.

momo
PAPIS
THEYS
30
DORAN
EXXON
LATI
Hella
LISTA
YOKOHAMA
momo
brembo
momo
EXXON

# PREFACE

By Jonathan Ingram

One of the key turning points of IMSA's topsy-turvy 1990s was the arrival of the incomparable Ferrari 333SP. Launched in 1994, the Italian steed was a major player among the World Sports Cars that helped define that era of IMSA. Making their highly anticipated debut at Road Atlanta, three of the scarlet red Ferraris took the green flag. After introducing fans to the audacious high-pitched note of their V12 engines, the Ferrari of Jay Cochran emerged as the winner just ahead of Gianpiero Moretti, godfather of the 333SP.

As the post-race celebration began, I started looking around the paddock for the president of Ferrari North America to get comments needed for a race report that would appear in *On Track* magazine. I soon found Gianluigi Longinotti-Buitoni on the hill behind Victory Lane near a stand of pine trees holding something next to his ear that looked like a shoe with a short antenna. In rapid-fire Italian, he was calling Maranello on one of the first cell phones I had ever seen to report the 333SP's inaugural victory.

Looking back, it can be difficult to recall how communication technology was relatively limited in the 1990s. The IMSA races were not regularly televised. Although portable computers like the Tandy 200 sold by RadioShack were readily available, the Internet was in its infancy. There were few, if any, cell phones—unless you bought a Consulier, which came equipped with one in the console. Most often fans learned about races through reports in newspapers or magazines long after the fact.

Who's fastest? Who's winning? And who won? The best way to keep up with those questions in real time was to buy a ticket, brave the elements, and show up at the track.

The book you are about to read is in many ways like having a ticket to the entire decade of IMSA racing in the 1990s, with one significant exception. Longtime IMSA officials Mark Raffauf and George Silbermann take readers behind closed doors and into the sanctioning body offices that witnessed five different owners during this tumultuous decade.

There are inside stories about the owners, the major sponsors, the logistics of street racing, controversies like fuel testing, and more.

In addition to the accounts of important episodes by these two executives, other key players from the decade were invited to contribute their experiences, including team owners, drivers, and car builders. Their stories bring additional insights to the hard-fought racing and the distinctive cars of the 1990s.

With a bevy of major turning points more often seen in an epic novel, IMSA survived as well as thrived during the topsy-turvy decade of the 1990s. The result for readers is an engaging, no-holds-barred saga featuring a variety of voices and perspectives about a decisive decade in American sports car racing.

As the saying goes, someone should write a book!

36
MICHELIN
JMR
motorbet.com

# INTRODUCTION

By Mark Raffauf

IMSA and professional sports car racing in North America underwent an extraordinary transformation during the 1990s.

Thanks to the leadership of founder John Bishop from 1969 to 1989, IMSA became one of the most successful sports car racing series in the world. But the stability of Bishop's steady command, girded by the long-running sponsorship from the Camel brand of R. J. Reynolds, soon gave way under multiple new owners and sponsors, followed by changes in the philosophy of sports car racing itself.

Cars that were very different from the previous twenty years would change the direction and future of the sport in a short period of time. By the end of the decade, as reflected by the cars, the groundwork was created that led to two different philosophies and two separate racing series. These two competing series embodied opposite approaches to technology and economics, each critical to success in motorsports.

One was based on the American racing business philosophy of structured costs, which Bishop's IMSA had always tried to be. The rival series was an American version of the European philosophy, where the technology often trumped cost considerations. Eventually, the two series converged in 2014 and the approach of Bishop returned under the direction of Jim France.

A race sanctioning body has three critical elements: principles (regulations); integrity (the ability to manage fairly the stated principles); and a reliable staff (honesty and transparency). Damage any of these elements and you risk spinning out of control.

During the 1990s, American professional sports car racing teetered on the brink of going out of control several times. Throw in geopolitical crises such as oil shortages, an overseas war, and a domestic economic downturn; yet, sports car racing thrived and evolved in a positive way.

That's a testament to the IMSA staffers who toughed out the turmoil for most of the 1990s with a good understanding of the way IMSA should be administered. Reinventing the wheel was never an option. History had already confirmed what would work.

Through it all, the racers entered and raced. They introduced new cars, new ideas, and new technologies, always putting on a good show for the thousands of fans who attended the events. TV coverage evolved. International influence grew when IMSA assisted racing neighbors in Europe, the Caribbean, and Japan.

As the sport navigated its way through the turbulence and change, the dedication, strength, and passion of the participants, the tracks operators, the sponsors, and the fans made progress possible.

To those who experienced the 1990s, this chronicle may bring back both good and bad memories. Those years led us to where the sport is in 2025—as strong as it has ever been. Thank you to all!

TOYOTA
99
TOYOTA
99
TOYOTA
TOYOTA
NISSAN
84
NISSAN
84
NISSAN
GTP ZX-TURBO
NISSAN
GTP ZX-TURBO
GOODYEAR
TRICK

CHAPTER ONE

# 1990: THE MOMENTUM CONTINUES

As the sun rose on February 4, 1990, the beginning of the International Motor Sports Association's (IMSA) third decade found two of the Jaguar XJR-12s of Tom Walkinshaw Racing (TWR) contesting victory in the season-opening 24 Hours of Daytona.

The favored 1989 championship-winning Nissan GTP ZX-Turbos had faded with reliability issues, Toyota's Eagles were overheating, and the venerable Porsche 962s had been pushed to their limits. The GTP cars of this era were capable of amazing outright speed—but not for twenty-four hours. Engines and brakes had to be managed to reach the finish. Because the cars physically abused the drivers with high downforce and dramatic vertical and horizontal g-loads, at least three (and often four) drivers were required to compete successfully. Teams often kept one driver fresh for early Sunday morning in case the cars survived the night and had to be raced hard for position after sunrise.

When dawn arrived, it was the two Jaguars powered by massive V12 engines that continued to duel until the final hour when the car of Price Cobb, John Nielsen, and Martin Brundle was slowed by overheating problems. The sister car driven by Davy Jones, Jan Lammers, and Andy Wallace powered past—their V12's distinctive screaming exhaust still at full song—to take the victory and complete a one-two finish for Tom Walkinshaw and his TWR team under sunny Florida skies at the Daytona International Speedway.

The annual icebreaker for circuit racing, the race marked the outset of another IMSA season of leading automotive brands and drivers battling on major North American circuits in the Camel GTP, Camel Light, GTO, and GTU series, each showcasing the latest technologies in their respective classes.

Despite this balmy season-opening occasion, there were ominous clouds on the horizon for IMSA. From the point of view of hindsight, it seemed

The Toyota HF89 and Nissan's GTP ZX-Turbo were not victorious at Daytona. *Brian Cleary*

fitting for the sanctioning body to be presiding over classic endurance events for sports cars, because IMSA would face ten years of daunting challenges that tested the sanctioning body's endurance. Over the course of a decade, it would undergo five turnovers in ownership, start up the new World Sports Car category, and locate a successor to the Camel brand's longtime title sponsorship due to federal policy changes on the promotion of tobacco products.

Just as the drivers, teams, and factories rose to the myriad challenges of racing, IMSA also experienced continued success over this long haul after many behind-the-scenes machinations to sustain the series founded by John Bishop, whose saga is told in the book *IMSA 1969–1989: The Inside Story of How John Bishop Built the World's Greatest Sports Car Racing Series.*

Early in 1989, he sold the sanctioning body to Mike Cone and Jeff Parker. The new owners were already investors behind the GTE World Challenge of Tampa and had been introduced to Bishop as possible buyers of IMSA during the 1988 season, a time when Bishop was looking to leave behind the daily grind of running a sanctioning body and was receiving a variety of queries.

A review of the accounting books by Cone and Parker had revealed IMSA's strong cash flow and cash reserves. In addition to making a solid

The Bayside Racing Porsche 962 of pole-winner Bob Wollek and the Nissan GTP ZX-Turbo of NPTI led the field into a new decade at the Rolex 24. *Brian Cleary*

Brother can you spare a front cowling? Fully prepared spare bodywork was a necessity. *Brian Cleary*

financial offer, the duo had one other important qualification: although they had helped promote the event in Tampa and had driven in Firestone Firehawk races, they were not regular racing participants.

Philosophically, Bishop was against the idea of competitors owning or organizing sports car endurance racing's only professional show. "That kind of structure would be like inmates running the asylum," he said. "Team owners that also owned the overall show would naturally have conflicts of interest at almost every level of the sport."

Throughout the sales process, the IMSA Board of Directors had one guiding principle during its discussions: do what was best for John and Peg Bishop. It was their blood, sweat, and tears that had built IMSA into a thriving business. They reasoned the Bishops deserved to reap the rewards of their labor and accepted a very good offer from Cone and Parker.

But competitors and many other participants in IMSA knew little about the two businessmen who had remained in the background during the two ill-fated and sparsely attended IMSA races in Tampa that were managed by Hal Kelley, who had persuaded Cone and Parker to look at buying IMSA.

Cone was a second-generation executive at Cone Construction, one of the ten largest road-building companies in the state. Parker was the son of the owner of the Pepsi bottling concern in Tampa and was a part-owner himself.

The deal to buy IMSA was finalized in February 1989, at which point Bishop resigned as the president. The purchase agreement kept Bishop on as a consultant and advisor for one year, with the idea that he would guide the new owners, provide important historical context, and help them take over relationships that had been carefully cultivated over many years, relationships that would be vital to the smooth running of IMSA and continued growth of the organization.

Bishop's departure and the first year of ownership by Cone and Parker resulted in problematic changes to the sanctioning body's internal operating procedures. But outwardly, the economic health and success of IMSA continued. In 1990, the Camel GT Series paid out more than $4.7 million in purse and point funds across all the prototype and GT categories. Average event attendance was reported by Goodyear Tire & Rubber Company to be 57,000, and

The Castrol Jaguars of Tom Walkinshaw Racing and their V12s outlasted all challengers to finish one-two, bringing the team a second Rolex 24 win in three attempts. *Peter Gloede*

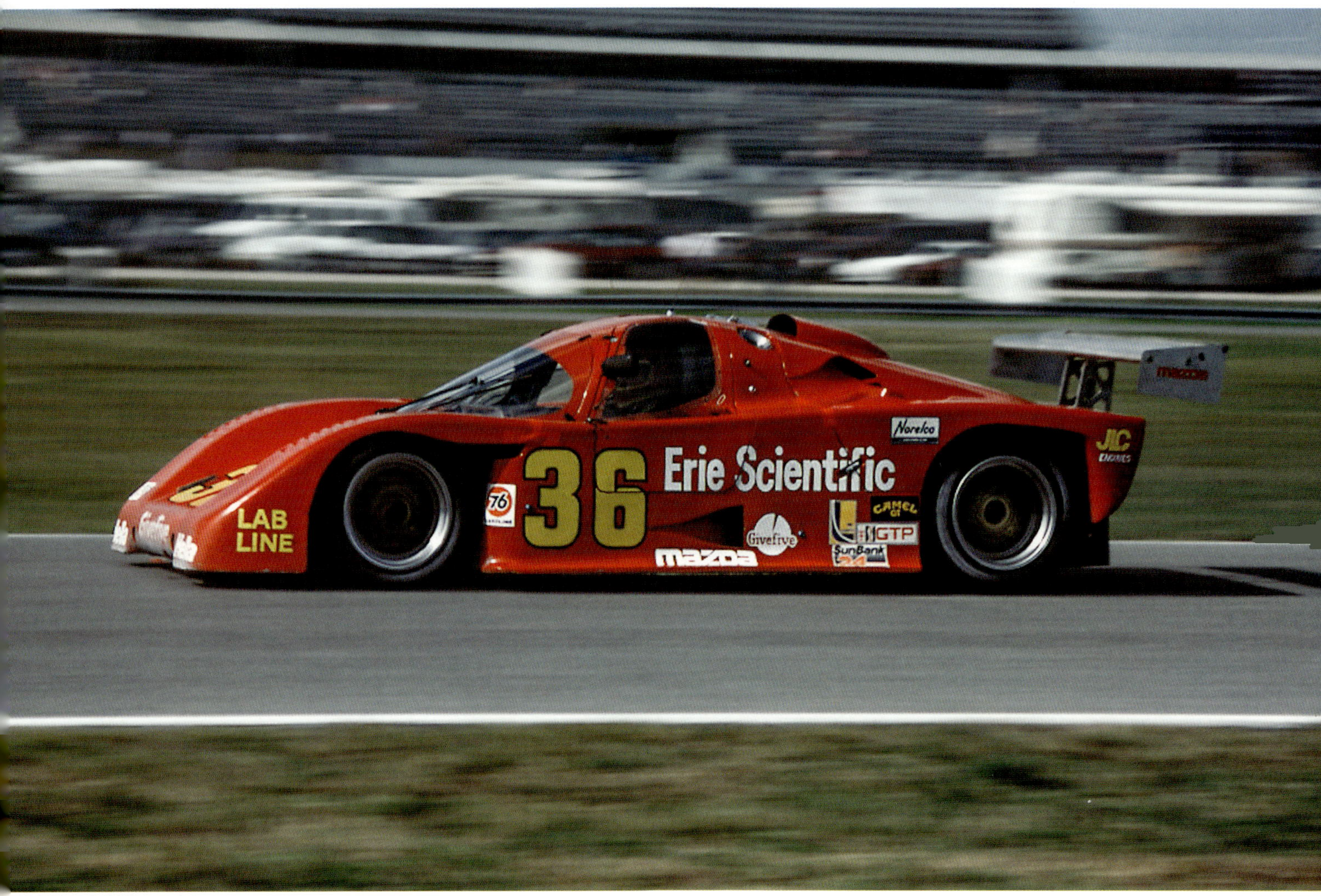


Powered by a Mazda 13B rotary, Erie Scientific drivers John Grooms, Michael Greenfield, and Frank Jellinek Jr. scored a Camel Lights victory on board an Argo JM16. *Peter Gloede*

yearly TV numbers topped 78 million viewers across all IMSA series event broadcasts.

On the track, the Camel GTP division featured continued growth and tougher competition than the previous six years. The drama included several milestones as both new GTP cars and existing designs arrived in Victory Lane.

The mid-season introduction of the Nissan NPT-90 resulted in five wins and a third consecutive championship for Geoff Brabham. The Dan Gurney–built Eagle HF89 Toyota won its first race at the inaugural appearance of the Camel GT Series at the Heartland Motorsports Park in Topeka, Kansas, with a flag-to-flag victory by Juan Manuel Fangio II over Brabham and Chip Robinson, who were teammates at Nissan Prototype Technology Inc. (NPTI). With the purse money and a Camel Pyramid bonus, Fangio was handed a check for $90,000 on the podium for the inaugural win. Three more wins during the second half of the season by Fangio in this Eagle helped pave the way for the soon-to-arrive MKIII.

Four different GTP manufacturers won races over the season due to an upset of sorts by James Weaver in the Porsche 962C of Dyson Racing in Tampa. A seven-year-old design, it was still capable of winning by a margin of almost two minutes after smart pit strategy decisions and brilliant driving by Weaver in the changing wet conditions.

Counting the two different winners from Jaguar (the V12 XJR-12 and the V6 turbo XJR-10) and two from Nissan (the GTP ZX-Turbo and NPT-90) plus wins by the Toyota HF89 and a Porsche 962C, six different car types turned in victories. The regulatory stability of the GTP category was confirmed.

A world-class competitor and factory Porsche driver, Derek Bell won regularly in the US and internationally. *Peter Gloede*

Weaver was always a threat in a Dyson Porsche, especially on street courses. He was leading the San Antonio race in the final laps when the slippery street course caught him out, along with just about every other front-runner. Two late race spins resulted in a fantastic battle between Robinson and Fangio, resolved in favor of Fangio when Robinson spun out as well.

The American V8-powered Spices also had moments of glory. Newcomer Perry McCarthy grabbed the pole at the Sears Point Raceway near Sonoma, California, in the entries run by Julian Randles. The 6.0-liter GM V8s were able to beat the factory turbo cars on speed at numerous events but were denied a victory despite several strong podium finishes. Al Unser Jr. claimed the pole on the Del Mar temporary circuit in the No. 33 Spice, but a miscue by co-driver Jay Cochran in traffic denied the fastest team a victory.

The TWR Castrol Jaguar squad led by Tony Dowe took two additional wins with the XJR-10 in addition to the Walkinshaw team's V12-powered victory at Daytona. Although not victorious, other notable performances came from Gianpiero Moretti in the MOMO-backed Porsche 962C; the works V8 Spice driven by Bernard Jourdain; and the first customer Nissan GTP ZX-Turbo of Jim Busby sponsored by BFGoodrich. These entries had competitive drives throughout the season, scoring poles and podiums, but alas no wins.

Brabham's third consecutive driver championship brought in over $350,000 in prize and point fund money. When Robinson and Bob Earl co-drove to victory at the Watkins Glen International six-hour event, they received a season-high $100,500 in purse and Camel bonus money, an amount that continued to inspire envy from other sports car racers for years to come.

The Camel Lights division, where Mazda rotaries, Buick V6 engines, and Ferrari V8s were the

Geoff Brabham in his office during what would become his third straight Camel GTP championship.
*Lee Self*

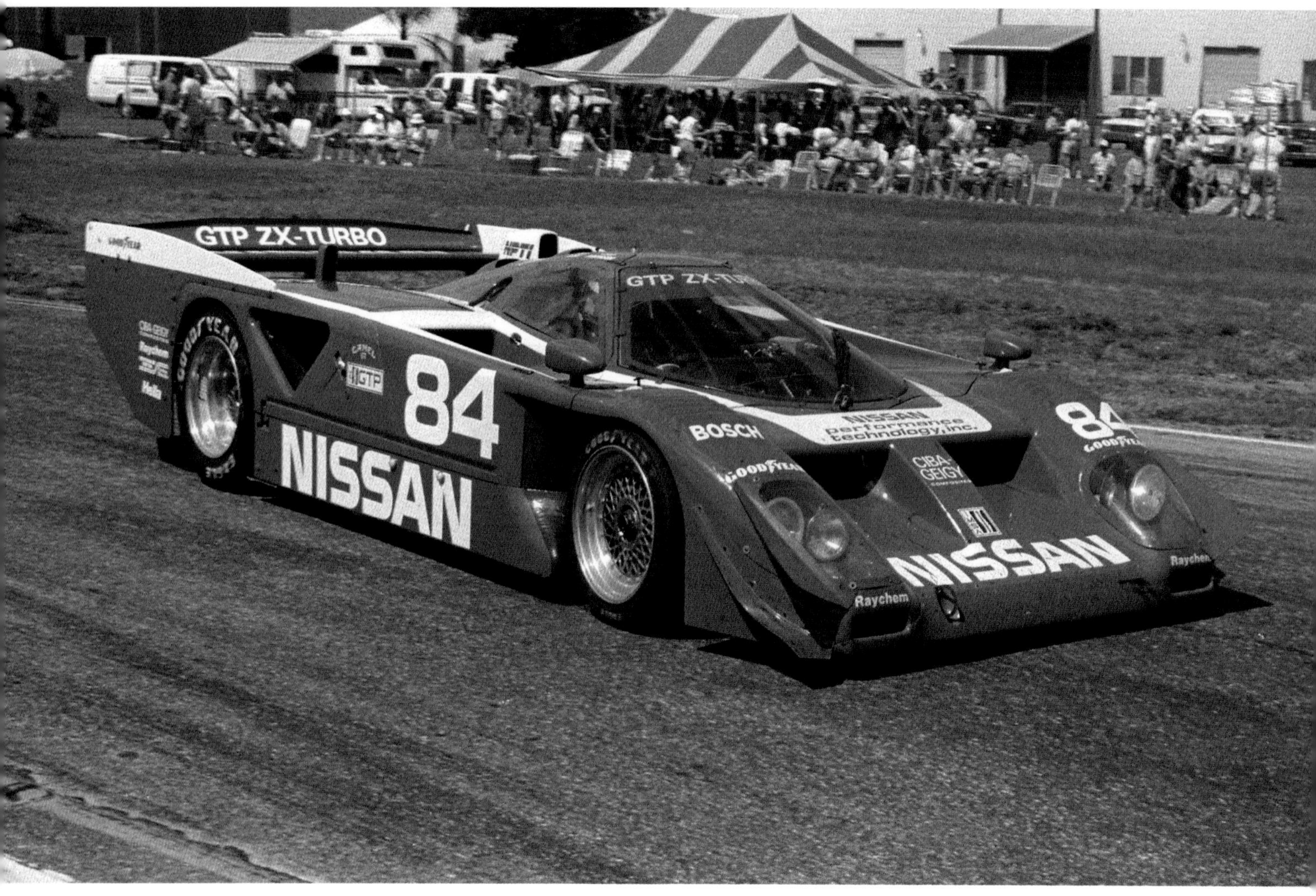


The Nissan of drivers Derek Daly and Bob Earl en route to victory at Sebring on the old Hangar Straight. Note the lack of barriers. *Bill Tuttle*

power plants of choice, also featured tough-to-win competition in 1990. At Daytona, a Mazda twin rotary-powered Argo won the smaller, less powerful Camel Lights prototype class, a career highlight for drivers John Grooms, Michael Greenfield, and Frank Jellinek Jr.

In the division's championship chase, the V6 Buick-Spice of Mexican driver Tomas Lopez got a strong challenge from the 3.0-liter V8 Ferrari-Spice of Ruggero Melgrati, who co-drove with car owner Martino Finotto to four victories. The Italian pair shadowed Lopez for the entire season in pursuit of the title. But the driver sponsored by Canada Shoes—made in Mexico no less—captured seven wins under the direction of team manager Randles, who rotated co-drivers all season. That gave Buick the manufacturer championship as well. The shape of things to come arrived with a victory by the CompTech team's Pontiac-Spice in the final round at Del Mar. Though presented in Acura's brilliant orange and white livery, the car ran with a Pontiac four-cylinder engine. With its new V6 Acura engine developed in house and ready to come online for 1991, CompTech and driver Parker Johnstone would become the team to beat.

An overflow crowd jammed Road Atlanta to watch the Camel GT. *Lee Self*

## GT Class Loses Sponsor, Gains 7/8ths Car

For the only second season since the early 1970s, the GT cars gathered at Daytona in 1990 for the first race without a title sponsorship. The looming departure of the Camel cigarettes brand at the end of the 1993 season—due to anticipated changes in federal law around cigarette advertising—led to a decision by the R. J. Reynolds Tobacco Company to concentrate sponsorship on the two prototype classes, and it dropped the GT classes. The company's officials pared back sponsorship to just the headline GTP series and Camel Lights in anticipation of what became the Tobacco Master Settlement Agreement in 1998, which limited tobacco companies' sports sponsorships and eventually banned them completely.

John Paul Jr. turned in some magnificent drives at the wheel of the BFGoodrich-backed Nissan, but he came up short of Victory Lane. *Peter Gloede*

At first glance, there was not much change in the GT class cars on the track. Team owner Jack Roush scored his sixth consecutive GTO win at Daytona for Ford/Lincoln Mercury with Robby Gordon, Lyn St. James, and Calvin Fish wheeling a Mercury Cougar XR-7 built in Roush's prolific

Rain did not slow the field at Road America.
*Peter Gloede*

Michigan shops as a replacement for the Merkur XR4Ti.

But there was a significant change underway. Introduced for the 1989 season, the XR-7s were referred to internally by IMSA as the 7/8th cars. Little known at the time, IMSA allowed manufacturers to reduce the size of the car bodies to fit the required maximum wheelbase of 108 inches on the standardized tube frame GT chassis. The Detroit manufacturers were building larger front-wheel-drive production cars, which resulted in long wheelbases and short overhangs in the front and rear. This included rear-wheel-drive cars like the XR-7. If the rear axle was simply moved forward to fit IMSA's shorter 108-inch wheelbase requirement, the rear wheels ended up in the door.

In cooperation with Ford's aerodynamicist Don Hayward, and with full supervision by IMSA, the entire car was scaled down to represent the Cougar and yet be competitive in the GTO class. The XR-7s were shorter, lower, and wider than the production car, but perfectly proportioned to the extent that nobody really noticed! They looked great, worked well, and were one of the more popular GT cars of the era. They were all done within the regulations with a process put forth to any manufacturer making a similar request. Later, GM's Oldsmobile Cutlass and Aurora would receive similar treatment, creating a generation of iconic 7/8th cars found only in IMSA.

When the GT season opened, there were two firsts at Daytona involving veteran driver Amos Johnson. Entering his third decade of competition, he co-drove to a runner-up finish in the GTO class behind the winning Cougar in the competition debut of the Lee Dykstra–designed Mazda RX-7, the first IMSA racer powered by a four-rotor engine. Johnson also entered his already successful Daytona-winning RX-7 in GTU, this one equipped with the venerable Mazda two-rotor engine. It scored the class victory in the hands of Peter Uria, Jim Pace, Bob Dodson, and Rusty Scott.

Jim Busby's team servicing the BFGoodrich Nissan during the Rolex 24. *Peter Gloede*

The season-long drama in the GT categories included numerous strong finishes by the spectacular Ferrari F40 that competed in GTO with a variety of world-class Formula One and sports car drivers piloting the beautiful red Italian entry. A switch from Pirelli tires to the more suitable Goodyear tires developed for US tracks lit up the car's performance, making it a potential winning combination each time it was entered. Former French Formula One drivers Jean-Pierre Jabouille, Jacques Laffite, Jean-Louis Schlesser, and Alain Ferté drove for team manager Jean Sage, who had managed the Renault Formula One team. Two appearances were made by American star Hurley Haywood. The crowd-pleasing big red machine scored second-place finishes in GTO at Mosport Park, Road America, and Watkins Glen, a third at the Mid-Ohio Sports Car Course, and a ninth at Lime Rock Park out of only seven starts.

Mercury Cougar won the manufacturer championship with Dorsey Schroeder leading a Roush Racing one-two in the driver championship over potent Nissan 300ZX Turbo entries from Clayton Cunningham and a brace of new four-rotor Mazda

RX-7s. Pete Halsmer gave this fantastic new Dykstra design its first win at Heartland Motorsports Park and then added victories at Mid-Ohio and San Antonio.

There were many memorable battles during the season, especially on temporary circuits. In the Long Beach street race, Schroeder was leading when a traffic incident cost him his hood and some front-end damage. Halsmer passed him in the RX-7 before Schroeder returned to the charge with his damaged car and eventually won by 3.4 seconds. At the Meadowlands temporary course in New Jersey, Halsmer had a good lead until trying to lap Steve Millen in the Nissan 300ZX Turbo. Contact resulted in heavy front-end damage to the RX-7. Halsmer valiantly tried to hold off Robby Gordon in his Cougar and Jeremy Dale in the other Nissan on the last lap, but he lost to Gordon by 0.43 seconds.

Another notable performance in New Jersey came from Joe Varde in the Ford RS200, which was

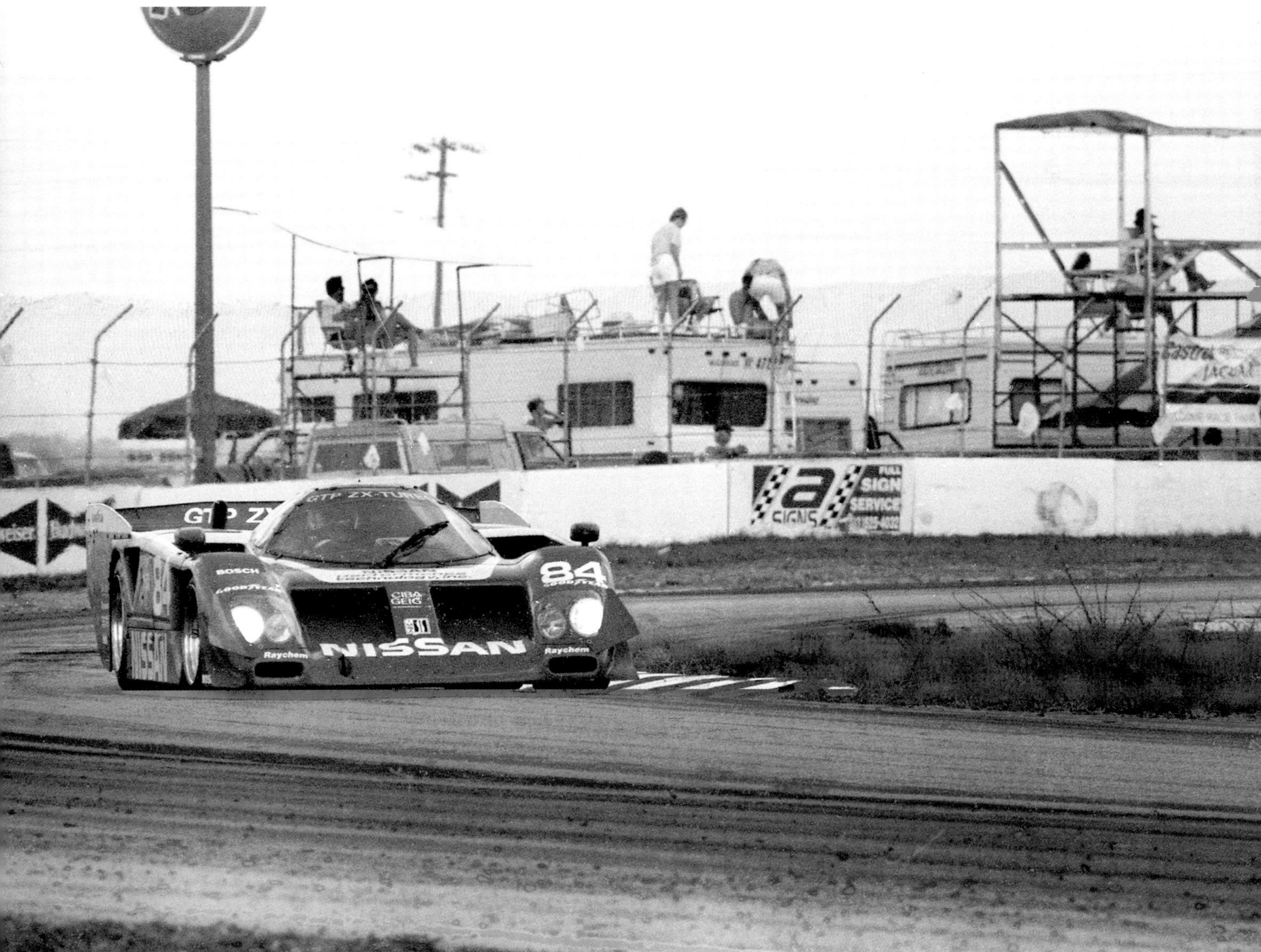


The twelve-hour distance at Sebring worked well for the V6 turbo of Nissan. The absence of sweeping allowed rubber to build up in the outside groove. *Brian Cleary*

Jim Miller's V8 Chevy-Spice became the first full-time ride in IMSA for Wayne Taylor. *Peter Gloede*

a road racing version of the Ford Group B rally car that was unique to IMSA. But mechanical woes in the all-wheel-drive car forced an early retirement after qualifying seventh. It appeared several times, but a heavy crash in San Antonio during practice ended the participation by this distinctive car.

Lance Stewart won the GTU drivers' title and helped clinch the manufacturer championships for the new Mazda MX-6 sedan with three wins and eleven top five finishes. After falling short at 24 Hours of Daytona, the Nissan 240SX of Bob Leitzinger bounced back with an unprecedented performance at 12 Hours of Sebring, winning by fourteen laps! By season's end, David Loring posted four convincing victories for Nissan in the Leitzinger entries. The Dodge Daytona entries of Full Time Racing took three wins in the hands of Don Knowles, who led a cadre of drivers from Chrysler in the little four-cylinder yellow and black bumble bees.

Historically, IMSA had always provided a place for American cars powered by V8 engines to showcase these vehicles and, as importantly, to offer privateers an affordable way to race professionally. In 1990, the Kelly American Challenge was renamed the All-American Challenge, a series that would race in conjunction with the GTO/GTU

The traffic at Daytona made it a challenging twenty-four-hour event. The bright arrow reminded drivers to turn at the bus stop. *Brian Cleary*

cars in the sprint events. The American V8 sedans drew competitors from the Kelly series as well as new entrants who found it an affordable option. The championship points ended in a tie between teammates Clay Young and Mark Porcaro, who each drove a red Pontiac Firebird. Young secured the title by virtue of four wins compared to his teammate's three.

Additional changes during 1990 included Tampa's temporary circuit becoming a Camel GT event after the ill-fated single World Challenge race the previous year for Group C and GTP cars that offered no points. This event—along with races in Miami, West Palm Beach, San Antonio, and Del Mar—gave the schedule five temporary course events for GTP and Lights. The GT class would compete at those venues in separate races from the prototypes. IMSA partnered with Championship Auto Racing Teams (CART) for the first time to share one of its series on a CART race weekend, resulting in two additional events for the class at Long Beach and the Meadowlands.

Entry-level series were an integral and important part of the original master plan for IMSA. They were devised by founder Bishop to revolutionize sports car racing by moving away from an image of exclusivity. Since its beginning, the long-held goal was to provide a multilevel platform of racing series that progressed in economic, technical, and skill levels to provide access to the sport to as many participants as possible. Throughout the 1970s and 1980s, these entry level programs proved their value due to the number of individual drivers, teams, manufacturers, businesses, and sponsors who progressed from the entry level to the top.

The first half of the 1990s carried some existing series to new heights in performance and even spawned a new series. This was reflective of an automotive industry undergoing changes in the types of cars manufactured, their technology, and tires. Changes in marketing and the activation of consumers were occurring as well.

International Sedans (IS), sponsored by Luk Clutches, was a mix of slightly modified sedans that represented manufacturers' lower-end performance vehicles, including front-wheel and rear-wheel

With Hans Stuck at the wheel, the Alucraft Porsche 962 looked flawless thanks to John Shapiro and his crew.
*Peter Gloede*

Driver John Nielsen and his TWR crew ready for a hot day in Miami. *Bill Tuttle*

drive. BFGoodrich and Toyo Tires competed head-to-head, and their drivers included future prototype stars Johnstone and Butch Leitzinger, plus veterans Dennis Shaw, Garth Ullom, and Scott Hoerr. Ullom won the 1990 championship in an Eagle Talon fielded by Paul Rossi, while Acura, Nissan, and Mitsubishi also tallied wins in the ten-race series.

The big elephant in the street tire racing world was the well-established Firestone Firehawk Endurance Series. Launched in 1985, it featured stock street cars with added safety features. It was divided into three categories based on street specifications, and its accessibility generated huge fields, started many driving careers, and eventually put over one million trouble-free competition miles on Firestone's Firehawk street tires. Notable participants over the years included Jeff Purner, Bob Akin, John O'Steen, John Heinricy, Andy Pilgrim, Boris Said, Terry Earwood, Varde, Weaver, and future GTO champion Schroeder, plus countless others who remained part of the fabric of sports car racing for many years. The Grand Sports, Sports, and Touring classes showcased real vehicle performance and provided many hours of close competition for fans.

The Firehawk version of street stock racing tested the endurance and speed of unmodified street cars and teams' abilities to fix them on the fly. Entertaining to watch and to participate in, the racing for position was ferocious, with constant action on (and sometimes off) the pavement.

The first event featuring all three Firehawk categories launched the 1990 season at Sebring and had such a massive entry that two separate races were needed. Sixty-nine cars started the four-hour Sports and Touring race and an additional fifty-five Grand Sports cars started a second four-hour race.

Later in the year, seventy-one cars from all three classes took the green flag in the twenty-four-hour race at Watkins Glen.

At a support race for the NASCAR weekend later in the year at Watkins Glen, another milestone occurred during the ninety-minute race held on the 2.2-mile short course. John Petrick qualified on the pole averaging over 100 miles per hour in a street stock unmodified Chevrolet Camaro, and Doug Goad almost matched it in the race with a fastest lap of 99.8 mph on shaved standard street tires. Nobody ever thought street cars of the time would go that fast with just the interior carpeting removed and a bolt-in roll cage.

The roll cages had to be removed completely and reinstalled on demand upon technical inspection to insure they were not welded into place for greater chassis rigidity. Once removed, the race car

With sparse track lighting, drivers used angled side lights to help judge their distance from the Daytona wall.
*NASCAR Archive and Research Center*

The Ferrari F40 GTOs at Lime Rock, the only race where two were entered. The factory team earned four podiums from selected entries. *Randy McKee*

became a street legal car again, except for the open exhaust pipes. This series provided the opportunity for many people to get involved and enjoy motor racing in an economical, organized, and safe way. It proved the quality and performance of many makes and models. If necessary, you could build an entry overnight in your home garage.

The Barber Saab Pro Series continued as IMSA's only open-wheel series. It featured identically prepared Mondial formula cars fitted with production Saab 900 Turbo engines and had been a starting point for professional drivers since its inception. The notables from 1990 included Rob Wilson, Bryan Herta, Walt Bohren, Kelly Collins, P. J. Jones, Mike Shank, and Pace—all of whom would move on to make their mark in major series among the ranks of drivers and team owners.

## PARADIGM SHIFT BEHIND THE SCENES

By George Silbermann

*George Silbermann got dragged to his first race by Mark Raffauf in the fall of 1974. College roommates at the University of Florida, they were soon working IMSA events as weekend warriors at the nearby Daytona and Sebring tracks as well as at Road Atlanta. After graduation, George continued to work on a weekend warrior basis before becoming a full-time employee.*

*He brought IMSA's timing and scoring into the computer age using RadioShack TSR-80s in 1982, leaving the classic labor-intensive pencil and paper process behind. He created and operated the hugely successful Firestone Firehawk Endurance Series for over a decade, then added the Bridgestone Supercar Series. He evolved into being IMSA's contract manager, negotiating all the sponsorship and sanction agreements that were constantly in the works.*

*In the 1990s, Silbermann and Raffauf managed the sanctioning body under various new owners, whose lack of experience brought directional uncertainty. Following the dismissal of Hal Kelley by owner Charlie Slater, George became the organization's president. His knowledge about IMSA, its operations and history, particularly the tumultuous decade of the 1990s, was unparalleled.*

At the time of the IMSA sale to Tampa businessmen Mike Cone and Jeff Parker in 1989, IMSA had amassed seven-figure reserves as part of its business portfolio, more than adequate to cover operating accounts for any foreseeable needs.

The reserves had been accumulated over many years under the watchful eyes of owners Peg and John Bishop, serving as more than a nest egg. The funds enabled IMSA to get through the ups and downs of its routine business cycles. Licensing revenues, for example, usually arrived at the beginning of the year, but award, banquet, and point fund expenses hit in the last quarter, which could lead to shortfalls when relying entirely on regular cash flow. Other revenues and expenses had varied timelines during the season. The reserves comprised a "safety net," used judiciously and only if needed.

After the completion of the IMSA sale, all the reserves and nearly all the operating capital in the IMSA bank accounts were transferred to the new owners. The funds were not spent on any IMSA functions, and they were never replaced. By the end of that first year of new ownership, just in time for the 1989 holiday season, IMSA was not able to make payroll.

It became clear this was more than a "timing issue" or a one-time hiccup. It was the new business reality. The constant need for the owners to infuse operating capital to cover routine expenses led to putting off necessary investments and sometimes delaying payables—including things like prize money. This was the backdrop against which the second era of IMSA ownership began.

For staff members who had been with IMSA for years and who had made the transition to the new headquarters in Tampa, Florida, from Bridgeport, Connecticut, this change was like throwing a light switch. For the rest of the sports car world, the change took longer to manifest and become apparent outside the sanctioning body offices.

As time passed, exasperated racing competitors (particularly those who were less well funded) would call, wondering when they would receive their prize money or point fund checks. Staff morale was affected. The joke around the IMSA office was that you didn't want to be the last person to the bank to cash a paycheck. Promoters and series sponsors became increasingly uneasy, which would have a bearing on several of their future IMSA-related decisions.

To the outside world, this next IMSA era began with the Camel-supported GTP series still in its heyday. Event promoters continued to draw large crowds to IMSA races. Television coverage was strong. The change in environment for those who worked at IMSA presented challenges, but the new business paradigm did not become the overarching force in most of the day-to-day decisions for the sanctioning body.

IMSA continued as a respected, impactful sanctioning body with strong racing programs, innovative ideas, a depth of leadership experience, and a time-proven philosophy. As time passed, however, the new business reality became a more significant factor. The influence of the operating issues extended beyond the behind-the-scenes operation of the sanctioning body, influencing stakeholders, sponsors, the sports car industry in general, and ultimately racing itself.

The Camel GT made a big splash during two visits to the new Heartland Motorsports Park circuit in Topeka, Kansas. *IMSA Archive*

## MEETING THE NEW OWNERS

From Rob Dyson

*After starting in GT cars, Rob Dyson made a highly successful debut in IMSA's upper echelon when his Dyson Racing team won at Lime Rock in 1985 with a Porsche 962 in the team's first Camel GTP entry. Chairman and CEO of Dyson-Kissner-Moran, an international holding company, his passion for racing led to highly successful entries in GTP, World Sports Cars, LMP675, LMP1, and LMP2 over the course of three decades. In addition, the team competed in Daytona Prototypes prior to the merger of IMSA with the Grand-Am Series. Dyson served a stint on the board of the International Speedway Corporation, which owned multiple major American oval and road circuits and was founded by Bill France Sr., a co-founder of IMSA. The following is his recollection of his first encounters with IMSA's new-for-1990 owners.*

Rob Dyson won championships as a team owner and was a positive influence on the success of IMSA for over three decades. *Rick Dole*

"After Mike Cone and Jeff Parker acquired IMSA, I was invited down to meet with them. I flew to Tampa, where IMSA's headquarters had relocated from Connecticut. I sat down with them and said, 'Hey, what's your guys' background?'

"As I was sitting there, I realized that these two guys knew nothing about racing. They still had a remnant of the Camel funding, although it wasn't as robust as it had been. But they still had a piece of it. I think they thought that was going to be a cashflow influx forever. I realized that these guys were not racers. They had never raced. I didn't think that they had ever even gone to a race.

"It was Hal Kelley who called me to come down. While in Tampa, I said, 'Here's a couple of things you got to understand. Goodyear Tires supports this series. You know that you have a lot of good venues and you got to preserve the venues. You have to stay close to the France family, because they were IMSA's legacy owners. They know what's going on. You should lean on them to help you on any questions. And don't screw it up. But they didn't listen. I got, 'Blah, blah, blah, blah.'

"I knew that this new ownership was going to be flaky. What we did at Dyson Racing was compete in all the races.

"This was not the end of John Bishop's era, but I was kind of angry. I had a slight anger relapse about the way John and the IMSA stockholders sold it to Cone and Parker. When I'm sitting with these guys

The disciplined Dyson squad brought well-prepared and sponsored Porsche 962s to the GTP fray, such as this 1990 entry at Road Atlanta. *Lee Self*

listening to what they had to say, I realized it could have been me, team owners Bob Akin, Bob Tullius, and others, who really know what they were doing, who could have owned IMSA.

"I recognized at that time there may have been some aversion by the original IMSA stockholders to sell to a group of car owners. This was the time CART was being operated by ownership interests. But the problem with that was OK in my view. By not selling IMSA to team owners, it ensured an entrance to the dance by these clowns. Granted, they probably overpaid for it, but what bothered me was why the IMSA stockholders didn't even talk to us? Myself, Tullius, and Akin were very successful business guys and team owners. Why wouldn't that transfer?

"Cone and Parker ended up with the only sports car racing in town. At that time, there was no alternative. That was it and we had to put up with it."

ICI
Katech inc

CHAPTER TWO

# 1991: FACTORIES LEVEL THE PLAYING FIELD

There were several major developments in IMSA during the 1991 season, starting with a victory in the season-opening 24 Hours of Daytona by the team of Reinhold Joest. In rainy conditions, the crack German squad earned the only win of the year by a Porsche 962C, the iconic, eight-year-old design. But it was a big one! The 962C chassis was powered by a water-cooled, twin-turbo flat six. The chassis itself was essentially the same car that was powered by a single turbo, air-cooled flat six that first began competing in IMSA in 1984.

Joining co-drivers Henri Pescarolo, Bob Wollek, Frank Jelinski, and John Winter, Hurley Haywood scored his ninth victory in the major endurance classics at Daytona, Le Mans, and Sebring, which broke a tie with Jacky Ickx for the most combined wins at those three tracks. The victory was not the only high point for Porsche. Mario Andretti joined sons Michael and Jeff in a 962C to finish fourth among GTP entrants. This would be the one and only time Andretti and his two sons ever competed together.

After ongoing discussions with organizers at the Fédération Internationale de l'Automobile (FIA) and Le Mans, this Daytona race was the first to accommodate the IMSA GTP and Group C formulas. Group C engine specifications (fuel restricted) and Group C legal chassis (they had smaller aero tunnels than GTP) were allowed to compete for Camel GT championship points. IMSA's power-to-weight formula was equated to Group C's fuel formula, and fuel was regulated to a specified amount to account for the length of the race and a smaller fuel tank capacity.

Only one prominent GTP team, NPTI, chose this route and they brought two V8-powered R90C Nissans, which were designed for Group C competition, to contest the race. The team had determined

The business end of the Chevrolet Intrepid, which scored one victory in 1991. Misfortune interrupted several other opportunities. *Lee Self*

JOEST
PORSCHE
BOSCH
Shell
BLAUPUNKT
SACHS
BOSCH
Shell
J. WINTER
F. JELINSKI
H. PESCAROLO
H. HAYWOOD
7
GOODYEAR
Brumos

Reinhold Joest's team won the Rolex 24 at Daytona, claiming one of the final victories for the Porsche 962 in its eighth season of IMSA competition. *Peter Gloede*

their GTP ZX-Turbo, which had a V6 engine, would not be up to the task after analyzing its mechanical failures from the 1990 race. The R90C would prove to be effective, but not yet a winner.

Before the twenty-four-hour race got underway, there were several major new developments that proved pivotal for the sanctioning body's future: a new GTO/GTU series sponsorship from Exxon, the arrival of a new Bridgestone series that used high performance street radial tires, and a shift away from temporary/street circuits.

Jack Roush produced the best record of any team principal at Daytona, winning nine straight twenty-four hours in the GTO class. After a year off, he returned to win a tenth. *Peter Gloede*

Exxon was an excellent fit with Reynolds Tobacco's backing of the Camel GT prototypes because it sold cigarettes at its retail gas station convenience stores. More significantly, it introduced Exxon to a larger sports marketing role that encouraged consumers to use premium fuels in premium cars. This became significant when the Camel GT Series' sponsorship ended and Exxon was converted to the role of title sponsor for the prototypes and GT series. Exxon would become the sole racing fuel supplier of the series, which ultimately would resolve fuel issues that soon arose in the prototype series.

Following Daytona and the remarkable Porsche win, the Camel GT and the newly named Exxon Supreme Series began another season of close competition for the top step of the podium.

At the first sprint race at the Fairgrounds in West Palm Beach, seven different engine and GTP chassis combinations finished in the top seven, forecasting what would be a very competitive Camel GT season. Jones brought the Jaguar XJR-10 turbo back to Victory Lane. Wayne Taylor finished second in the debut of the new Bob Riley–designed Chevrolet Intrepid, ahead of Brabham in the NPT-90. Tommy Kendall, waiting for his new Intrepid, made his debut with the MTI Racing team in its older Chevy-Spice (the ex–Jim Miller/Taylor MTI chassis) and finished fourth. A Toyota Eagle earned fifth place, followed by the open-top Gunnar 962, often referred to as a 966, and the Joest Porsche 962C.

At Sebring, the twelve-hour event again proved to be the best endurance racing distance for Nissan, which returned to Victory Lane with the NPT-90. The remainder of the season was a steady grind for Brabham with only this one win, but plenty of top five finishes. Teammate Robinson won two races but fell short of Brabham's fourth championship

The American-flagged Ford Mustangs of Roush won another Camel GTO championship in 1991. They began life as Mercury Cougars. *Peter Gloede*

run by just five points, with Jones of Jaguar finishing a close third. By season's end, the five factory-supported brands of Jaguar, Nissan, Toyota, Chevrolet, and Porsche each won at least one race, making it the most competitive GTP season ever among both drivers and manufacturers.

The NPTI team updated to a GTP-91 chassis at Miami's street circuit, which helped Brabham maintain enough consistency to win the title with one race victory. Jones and the newly liveried Bud Lite Jaguar won six races, but the championship eluded the TWR team once again. Toyota posted three wins, including two by the Eagle MKIII, the latest design from All American Racers that would replace the HF90 at the Laguna Seca Raceway later in the year.

The Intrepids led at almost every race during the year with either Taylor or Kendall behind the wheel, but various miscues and mechanical issues, including Kendall's huge crash at Watkins Glen, left the promising MTI Racing team of Chevrolet and Jim Miller with only one victory, at New Orleans in June.

After Gurney's team unveiled the new MKIII at Laguna Seca, they promptly began an era of Toyota dominance in the hands of Fangio, who won one week later in Portland. The six wins between TWR drivers Jones and Raul Boesel came in three different GTP models throughout the season, the XJR-10, the XJR-12, and the new XJR-16.

Brabham survived a spectacular crash at Road America at the end of the summer and had to miss that event due to injuries, which opened the door for NPTI teammate Robinson. An apparent tire failure at close to 200 miles per hour on the front straight resulted in Brabham's car cartwheeling before coming to a rest in Turn One after scattering most of its componentry down the track. It took almost forty-five minutes to get him out of

Bob Wollek got the victory kiss. Looking on left to right: Reinhold Joest, Henri Pescarolo, Hurley Haywood, Frank Jelinski, and John Winter. *Peter Gloede*

Led by Jaguars and Nissans, the starting field prepared to unleash thousands of horsepower at Road Atlanta. *Lee Self*

the remains of the car. Luckily, although he was battered and bruised, it was not a life-threatening situation.

The always-consistent Brabham cruised to an unprecedented fourth consecutive Camel GTP championship at the season finale in Del Mar after Robinson and Jones both suffered mechanical failures.

Moretti and MOMO introduced a new Audi-powered Gebhardt GTP car, but it was never fully developed and struggled in its selected appearances. Team owner Tom Milner ran a pair of V8 Spices with Applebee's restaurant sponsorship and scored several top five finishes among the strong factory programs.

The CompTech Acura dominated Camel Lights, where Johnstone captured eight of the fourteen races, starting with a dominating twenty-two-lap victory in the twenty-four hour. Ferrari V8 Spices won four times, including two solo performances by Melgrati and one by David Tennyson, who paired with Ken Knott for a second win. The Essex Racing Kudzus powered by stalwart Buick V6 engines and driven by Charles Morgan and Jim Pace endured the bumps to win the 12 Hours of Sebring. Pace later scored a solo victory in the sprint race at Road America.

## EXXON: A GAME CHANGER

The newly named Exxon Supreme Series and a relationship with the gas and oil giant resulted from the guidance and advice of R. J. Reynolds officials, who introduced IMSA to Max Muhleman, a prominent sports marketing player from Charlotte, North Carolina.

Thanks to Muhleman's involvement, IMSA converted Exxon into a series sponsor from the company's existing position as a rear deck lid sponsor on NASCAR team owner Rick Hendrick's stock cars. Exxon began developing alternative event activation concepts, running TV advertisements built around racing, and created the first widely used high-octane, unleaded racing gasoline, which became the standard for the racing industry after just a few seasons.

GT again had three categories in 1991. GTO featured three factory teams, each with their own technologies that produced a championship hotly contested between Mazda, Nissan, and Ford. Under the direction of Jim Downing and his team, Halsmer and the now fully developed and potent four-rotor Mazda RX-7 won three races to win the inaugural Exxon Supreme GTO championship by only four points over Robby Gordon, who scored five wins in the Roush Racing Mustangs. The combined efforts of Millen and Dale produced five wins in the always competitive Cunningham Racing Nissan 300ZX Turbos, which helped Nissan tie Ford for second in the manufacturer points. But Ford finished second in the championship due to an overall victory total of six.

In GTU, John Fergus dominated the championship with eight wins out of the fifteen races he ran in his Dodge Daytona. Under the watchful management of Emory Donaldson at Full Time Racing and the masterful driving of the little four-cylinder entries by Fergus and two-time race winner Purner, the Daytona proved hard to beat. After initially starting with rear-wheel-drive and front-wheel-drive entries, the team decided to make their

The potent V6 twin-turbo Jaguar XJR-16. *Lee Self*

assault with two rear-wheel-drive Daytonas. Nissan drivers took four wins. A rotary Mazda won the season opening 24 Hours of Daytona again, this time with Dick Greer's Wendy's-sponsored RX-7, before cars powered by piston engines, began to dominate the races.

The All-American Challenge remained a solid portion of the new Exxon Supreme GTO fields. Camaros, Chevrolet Berettas, Oldsmobile Calais, and Buick Somersets brought plenty of action and noise from their V8s over the thirteen-race sprint championship held in conjunction with GTO and GTU. Greer took the championship at the final Del Mar round over 1973 GTO champion Phil Currin by a mere six points. Currin won five races to Greer's one but missed two, and it cost him a second IMSA championship.

The continuing success of the Firestone Firehawk prompted a new series with the branding of parent company Bridgestone. It followed the original series concept but called for higher performing cars, such as Porsche 911 Turbos, Corvettes, Lotus

Large rear wings helped extend the influence of ground effects tunnels while providing additional downforce and balance. *Lee Self*

Davy Jones conferring with team manager Tony Dowe. They teamed up for many wins in a variety of TWR Jaguars, but a championship eluded them. *Peter Gloede*

Esprit, Dodge Stealth, and the Consulier GTP. The odd car in the mix was the Consulier, conceived and built in South Florida by entrepreneur Warren Mosler. Quirky at best, it was surprisingly quick and handled great due to its light weight and good brakes. A little four-cylinder turbo Chrysler gave it enough guts to be scary. Stewart and Chet Fillip each won one race on board a Consulier, whose road-going versions were the first ever to have a built-in cell phone delivered with the car!

Regular Supercar series participants included world class drivers like Haywood, Fillip, Hans Stuck, Doc Bundy, Paul Newman, and Mike Brockman. Haywood won the inaugural seven-race series in a famous No. 59 Brumos Porsche 911 Turbo.

The Firehawk series stormed along with solid grids for the ten-race series with the showcase twenty-four-hour race at Watkins Glen growing in stature every year as the premier event that everyone wanted to win. The first Glen race of the 1991 season took place in June and started sixty-three cars representing the three classes. In August, sixty-seven cars started on the NASCAR weekend. At September's twenty-four-hour race, the green flag waved for seventy-nine cars—the largest starting grid in Watkins Glen history.

The International Sedan Series changed branding to the Toyo Tire Touring Series and the company became its exclusive tire supplier. Chuck Hemmingson in his Oldsmobile-supported 442 battled the Nissan 240SXs of Cass Whitehead, Butch Leitzinger, and Pepe Pombo, taking the championship with three wins to the collective four by the Nissan drivers. The writing was on the wall for the end of the series, unfortunately, as the tremendous success of the Firestone Firehawk series was rapidly eroding away the original concept of smaller cars competing on street radials.

The Barber Saab Pro Series once again showcased rising open wheel and sports car talent with

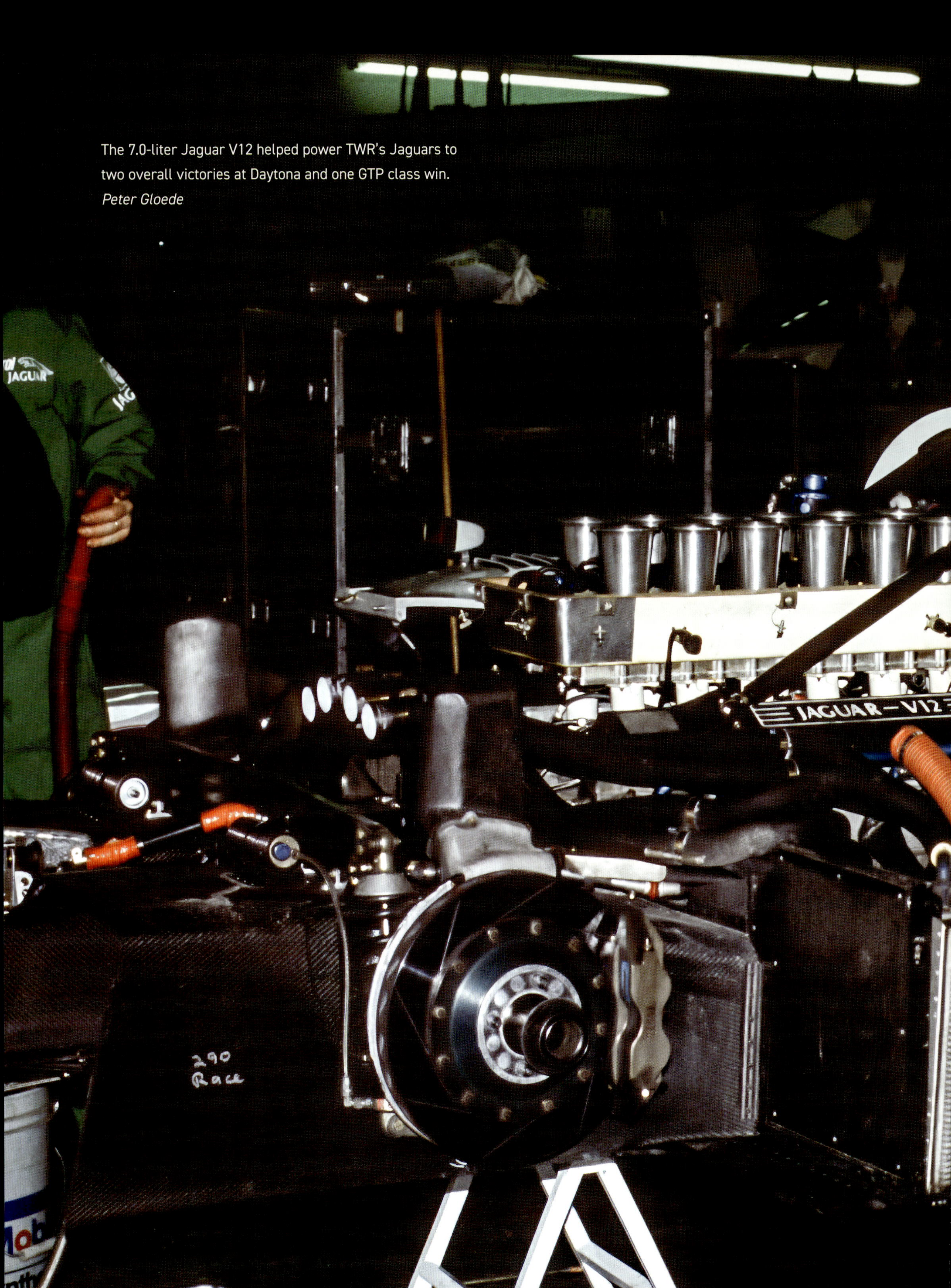


The 7.0-liter Jaguar V12 helped power TWR's Jaguars to two overall victories at Daytona and one GTP class win. *Peter Gloede*

PUSH
BUD LIGHT
DAVY JONES
SCOTT PRUETT
RAUL BOESEL
DEREK WARWICK
BUD LIGHT
JAGUAR
NEW PADS
JAGUAR

notables Herta, Jones, Todd Snyder, Riccardo Donà, and Johnny Robinson. Herta squeaked out the championship over twelve races, winning four and finishing on the podium in all but one. Despite seven victories, Robinson trailed him by three points in the championship.

The temporary circuits in San Antonio and the Florida State Fairgrounds in Tampa did not return to the schedule in the 1991 season for various reasons. A new event run on the streets of New Orleans would prove how difficult city circuits had become, and the realization began to sink in that the street course/temporary track era was coming to an end. There were four street courses on the schedule in 1991, three in 1992, and finally just one in 1993.

New Orleans proved to be the ultimate street racing challenge.

Poor planning, the lack of staff from the promoter, and a tough downtown location made the first race in New Orleans around the old convention center a logistical nightmare. By Wednesday, it was clear the event would not start the first practice session scheduled for Friday morning on time.

By then, most of the New Orleans operational staff had disappeared, leaving behind a race course that was far from finished. A small team of experienced IMSA staffers remained along with four experienced individual contractors who had been supporting IMSA at all the street races of the era.

By Friday afternoon, numerous staffers were driving and operating construction equipment for the first time, slinging 12,000-pound blocks for the barrier wall and dropping them into place with a forklift. Tire pack barriers were located and fences were installed—all in the summer heat and humidity. The work continued into the night without pause.

"The promoter had at least planned for a group of inmates from the New Orleans jail to come work for us," said Mark Raffauf. "We fed them shrimp po' boy sandwiches and sodas from a well-known local deli and they worked their asses off, happy to be outside their cells."

Fans and curiosity seekers, after a night of revelry, milled around the course-in-the-making all night long. They asked questions and wondered if it was ever going to come together. It was chaos for a while, but as the sun rose on Saturday the barriers and most of the spectator fencing was in place. The whole area was jammed with people, forcing spectator security to be redone. The fans had begun moving fences to get closer to the anticipated action in the streets.

Shortly after midday, the racing party was on. Engines roared and wheels turned in anger. The noise between the downtown buildings was spectacular. After a brief practice, three qualifying sessions for the classes of GTU, GTO, and GTP/Camel Lights were completed.

By race day on Sunday, IMSA was back on schedule. Spectators packed the place and the NBC broadcast started right on time—a good thing, because strong thunderstorms and lightning shortened the race a few laps. When it was over, the staff at IMSA looked around and collectively breathed a sigh of relief. What a mess it had been. The Big Easy was not easy!

Because of the construction of a new casino after the first year's race, subsequent events returned to a new course around the famed Superdome a few blocks up the street. A much more reasonable place to build a course around. The use of the floor of the Superdome by teams and their haulers was a big bonus. It ranks as one of racing's most spectacular paddock areas anywhere at any time—perhaps the most expensive and luxurious garage ever for a car racing event!

Outside of racing, the world was changing. A new Middle East war was brewing after the Iraqi invasion of Kuwait in August 1990, which put stress on the global oil economy. Automotive sales began dropping worldwide as oil prices rose to new heights due to the interruption of Middle

East supplies. Domestic auto sales dropped from a peak of 16 million units in 1986 to 12.5 million units by the end of 1990, subsequently increasing the stress on motorsports programs supported by manufacturers.

## CHANGES INSIDE IMSA

Inside IMSA, there were additional significant changes under the new ownership. Cone had bought out initial partner Parker and become the sole owner and CEO. The management team responsible for day-to-day operations and events was joined by Mike Huling, who moved into the marketing role at IMSA after working at the agency that managed car and motorcycle racing programs for British tire company Dunlop in the US. He was intimately familiar with the sanctioning body and the Camel GT through his work with the racing partnership of Jaguar Cars and Dunlop.

Huling began a successful run in both maintaining existing partnerships as well as bringing on new ones. He directed economically successful network TV packaging and special *USA Today* newspaper supplements, which broadened awareness of the Camel GT. Major progress was made during the year enabling IMSA to announce that energy giant Exxon was taking over the title sponsorship of the GT series in 1991.

The broader IMSA community, meanwhile, struggled with Cone. He clearly was not a racing enthusiast. Unlike his predecessor, who attended every race and was always available in the paddock, Cone rarely showed up at races. No one could figure out why he had bought the sanctioning body after being involved in the Tampa race with event promoter Hal Kelley. With limited racing background, Cone was no John Bishop, and the in-house IMSA management team had to go to great lengths to maintain the consistency and even-handedness that had been a hallmark of Bishop's ownership and management. Kelley, who operated in the wings as an advisor to Cone, was not a positive influence on the other event promoters and industry, often presenting himself as an IMSA official. His statements were sometimes contrary to what IMSA was doing. It was a difficult time.

By the end of the season, it became clear Cone's position of being both owner and CEO was not providing the expected stability and confidence within the racing industry. The years of 1990 and 1991 had been difficult internally, with financial shenanigans, misdirected marketing initiatives, staff problems, and unrealistic expectations keeping morale at its lowest point ever.

Several stern advisories to Cone came from industry leaders such as NASCAR President Bill France Jr., former owner Bishop, and International Speedway Corporation Executive John Cooper. In their respective roles, each of these men had a vested interest in the ongoing success of IMSA and none of them needed an invitation when it came to expressing their opinions. They could see Cone's daily leadership was lacking in racing industry expertise. He showed little concern for track promoters and those wishing to keep European sports car racing interests from meddling in the US market. Cone finally relented to the pressure and agreed to have Dan Greenwood become the new IMSA president. Along with racing industry leaders, the IMSA staff was fully supportive of having a buffer between Cone and the company.

Greenwood had served as vice president of the Los Angeles Olympic Organizing Committee before becoming the last president of Riverside International Raceway in Southern California. As NASCAR's liaison to the producers during the filming of *Days of Thunder*, he brought impeccable credentials to IMSA. Besides agreeing to hire Greenwood, Cone also agreed to a board of directors made up of himself, Bishop, Cooper, and Greenwood and started holding actual board meetings. This gave the leadership of the day-to-day staff additional allies and was greatly appreciated.

This T-shirt showcases comments heard on the radio network that connected IMSA's crew during preparations for the inaugural New Orleans street race. *Mark Raffauf Collection*

## URBAN MYTHS

By George Silbermann

In the 1960s, before the advent of cable television, a generation grew up watching auto racing on ABC's *Wide World of Sports*. In addition to the Indy 500 and Daytona 500, the third pillar of the sports anthology show's motorsports coverage was the Grand Prix of Monaco. There was something exotic about race cars dashing through city streets alongside the Mediterranean Sea.

In the US, street racing became all the rage from the early 1980s to the latter years of the 1990s. IMSA chose to ride this horse, despite occasional misgivings about some of the underlying business models and possible effects on permanent racetracks. On average, IMSA was approached every two to three months by a person or group claiming to have a great idea, an interested city, all the necessary backing, and so on. Maybe one in twenty of these great ideas led to additional discussions.

IMSA was not the only sanctioning body involved in racing on city streets and other temporary circuits during that heady era. Formula One held street races, all short-lived, in different American cities as it tried to regain a foothold in the US after losing events at the Watkins Glen circuit and the iconic Long Beach street race. CART, Champ Car, the Indy Racing League, and the SCCA all routinely had one or more temporary/street circuit races on their calendars during the period.

IMSA's hands-on experience with temporary circuits dated back to the original Miami Grand Prix, first held along the streets of that city's waterfront in 1983. By the time the Bishops sold IMSA in 1989, the Camel GTP series included five temporary circuits on that year's fifteen-race calendar. Races at temporary circuits would remain a factor on each IMSA calendar well into the rise of the Exxon World Sports Car era that began in 1994.

Street races were a glamorous, high-profile way to showcase a city and put it on the map. They were prestigious, drew widespread media attention, and looked extraordinary on television. From a practical standpoint, they also allowed motorsports events to take place in markets that did not have permanent racetracks. Sometimes it was seen as "taking the sport directly to the people," helping draw new fans to sports car racing.

There was certainly something exotic about conducting races in these city settings, and they usually resulted in lots of tremendous racing action and excitement. Behind the spotlights, there were real world considerations such as challenging business models, the difficulties of racing in an urban setting, as well as the occasional humorous moments. Here are two examples from different ends of the spectrum.

The final round of the 1989 Camel GTP season was held on a temporary circuit at the Del Mar Fairgrounds near San Diego, a venue that would continue as the setting for the series finale into the early 1990s. The driving force behind the event was Chris Pook, longtime promoter of the classic Long Beach Grand Prix. Often fondly described as a "character," he was also an innovator and a very shrewd businessman. Del Mar had some of the toughest requirements of any temporary racing venue at that time.

For example, a very small fluid spill in the paddock area one year triggered a high-level hazmat intervention that nearly shut the event down. Sound levels from the overall event and from individual cars on track were vigorously monitored and limits were strictly enforced. After getting cited and penalized more than once during the race, James Weaver wheeled his Dyson Porsche 962C through the corner near the monitoring station far too wide and nailed the freestanding sound meter microphone, putting it out of commission.

Pook was the master of organization for street races by way of his daily "crack-of-dawn" operational meetings. Attendance was mandatory for a wide variety of groups, including his staff, sanctioning body staff, and representatives from various local and state authorities. Everyone in the room was walked step-by-step through the detailed schedule for that day, ensuring the many operational moving parts were all accounted for and working in harmony. It may sound like a simple process, but it made a real difference in the staff's ability to handle the inherent complexities of street racing and the many unforeseen surprises that would invariably crop up.

Then there was the New Orleans street race. The "Big Easy" turned out to be far from easy when it came to street racing. Talk of voodoo dolls entered the conversation more than once.

To give you a taste of the "loosey goosey" environment, when Mark Raffauf and I made our initial preliminary visit prior to the 1991 race, it was supposed to have been extremely confidential and completely under the radar. No deal had yet been struck. As we stepped off the plane and came through the arrival gate, a New Orleans brass band greeted us along with a bunch of camera crews. We quickly sidestepped the passenger line and ducked out before being identified.

In New Orleans, it seems that everything gets done in time. Then again, maybe it doesn't, and you must roll with the punches. The night before the track was scheduled to open, construction of the temporary circuit was clearly way behind schedule. The available labor was inadequate for the task at hand. Almost the entire IMSA staff suddenly turned into construction workers and performed other needed roles. Most got zero sleep that night. Then they had to run and officiate a very challenging event starting the next day (once the track was finally assembled and ready) and through the ensuing long race day.

After the event, a limited-run, custom T-shirt was produced and sent to many of the key people who had been involved. It listed many of the bizarre or surreal radio exchanges that occurred between officials, track operational people, the promoter, and others during that weekend. Unless you had been behind the scenes, reading that T-shirt years later would be like trying to make sense of some lost language.

Street racing did not suddenly end when that era wound down. IMSA's 2021 schedule included three temporary circuits in the US as a companion to IndyCar, plus a support series presence at three temporary circuits in Canada with Formula One, IndyCar, and NASCAR. Formula One returned to street racing in the US in 2022 with an event in Miami. The FIA also sanctioned a Formula E event in New York City that featured a temporary circuit built on a cruise ship pier across the water from downtown Manhattan.

During the heyday of street races in America, IMSA played a leading role. Many of the safety standards, operational protocols, and important lessons learned from that era have resonated down through time and have a direct influence on the street racing of today.

## TAYLOR OFF TO FAST START IN AMERICA

From Wayne Taylor

South African Wayne Taylor first found success in the US when he drove for Spice Engineering in three IMSA races late in 1989 after driving one of the factory team's 3.5-liter Ford entries in Group C earlier that season. With no intentions of ever staying in the US, he won a pole in Del Mar and returned for the 1990 season to co-drive a Spice with team owner Jim Miller. Taylor's thirty-five-year career is a prime example of the opportunities presented by the IMSA platform. He moved from driver to champion to team owner, and he remains the only driver to win races in GTP, Camel Lights, World Sports Cars, Daytona Prototypes, and

After driving for the factory Spice team, Wayne Taylor's first regular IMSA ride was in Jim Miller's Chevrolet-Spice in 1990. *Peter Gloede*

The initial Intrepid season with teammate Tommy Kendall netted Taylor his first GTP win at the race in New Orleans. *General Motors / IMSA Archive*

DPi. He won team and driver championships in WSC, DP, and DPi while becoming one of the longest tenured competitors in the IMSA paddock. He entered the 2024 season as the co-owner of two factory-supported Acura ARX-06 GTP entries. The following comments are his recollections.

"I had been hired to come to the US in 1988 to drive at Daytona and it was an ADA Engineering sports car run by an English team. It was a bit of a fiasco. At that time, I didn't want to race in America, thinking, 'Those guys don't know what's going on out there. I want to be in Europe where it all happens.'

"I drove in Group C in 1989 in the Spice and at the end of the season I was asked about driving three races in the US by the team. That year's Del Mar race was $180,000 prize money for the winner! I got into the Spice USA program with Julian Randles, where he had drivers that brought money.

"I came over for the race at Sears Point with all those factory Nissans, Jaguars, and Toyotas. I can't recall what happened in Sears Point. It was just a normal race. But when I went to Tampa, I qualified on the second row of the grid. So, there was some attention towards me at that point.

"Then going to Del Mar, I put the Chevrolet Spice car on the pole and there were all the factory teams behind me. I was the only privateer-backed car along with Jim Miller, who was running the MTI Vacations Chevrolet Spice. Afterwards, I had approaches from Nissan and from Dan Gurney. Being loyal, I said, 'I don't think I can do that. I've got to see what Spice are going to do.' I was too naive at that time to understand that this racing was still going to cost money.

"We did those three races, and then it was up. Our son Ricky was born in England. My wife Shelley and I flew back to South Africa with him and said, 'What the heck are we going to do now?' And then I got a call from Jim Miller. He says, 'I've got a seat in my MTI Vacations car. Bob Earl is moving to Nissan, so I'd like to have you with me.' I had no money. I mean, no money. It was the first time I got paid instead of bringing a deal or sponsor. It was like $3,000 a race. So, I moved my entire family to the US for $3,000 a race.

"During 1990, we did well for a small team with top qualifying positions and a few podiums against all the factory teams and the Porsches. We had a great year and I just fell in love with racing in America. I thought, 'What are those idiots in Europe thinking?' The racing was competitive, maybe even more competitive. And it was just more open, and you could get things done.

"During the 1990 season, Jim told me that he was commissioning Bob Riley to design this new Intrepid GTP car, and he was going to try to get some General Motors support. He offered me double the amount of money. In the meantime, I'd committed to building a house and I still don't know to this day how they gave me a loan when I had no backing. I still don't know how that happened.

"In 1991, the Intrepid year started. And then, Chevrolet decided to run a second one with Kendall. They built the first Intrepid and they didn't have a second one for Tommy. He drove the Spice that Jim and I shared the previous year. We were both going to drive solo with no co-drivers.

"I got four poles that year and I won in New Orleans and Tommy got three poles, but he didn't win a race. And then he had that big accident at Watkins Glen. Given the size of the accident, which I could see the crews working on from behind the pace car, I thought 'Man, they've got to bring me into the pits. This is dangerous.' But they didn't bring me in. Then Jim called me up one morning and said, 'Look, I've got to give you a warning. GM is not going to renew its deal with me to have you next year. But don't worry about it. You can take this year's money to the bank, and you'll be fine, you can race all year.'

"Then I won the pole at the last race in Del Mar and was leading by the time I came in for the first pit stop and the clutch exploded. So that was my last race in a factory-backed Intrepid GTP car.

"In 1992, Parker Johnstone was running CompTech's Acura-Spice in Camel Lights, and because the team was using a Spice chassis I got a call. They said Acura was struggling in the championship. Buick was close in manufacturer points and the series was very competitive and they needed somebody in between. It was my first relationship with Acura. My job was to protect their position in the manufacturer championship. I drove with Ruggero Melgrati, recently the shoe in the very quick Ferrari-powered cars, and our first race was Laguna, and we won the race. I thought, 'Oh, shit. I'm not supposed to win.' It was like one of those things and they were all OK with it due to first place manufacturer points.

"Then in Del Mar, I did the job that they asked me to do. I have a big poster signed by everybody on the team saying they'll never forget, because I literally blocked everybody. I didn't care. My job was to do this. I braked, I let them hit me, I banged everybody, and I did my job, right? Parker Johnstone and Acura won the championships.

"In 1993, I really had to set this thing up where I was negotiating sponsorship deals and driving the car. Mike Gue ran the Intrepid for me that year. As far as race results were concerned, it was a disaster because the Intrepid was built to run on carbon brakes and we were on steel brakes. The car just couldn't compete.

"We had a couple of podiums, but it enabled me to get a proper sponsor for 1994 and a full season in the inaugural Exxon World Sports Car Championship. In those days, it was not a lot of money."

Achieva
mazda
HALE ENTERPRISE
GOODYEAR

CHAPTER THREE

# 1992: STORM CLOUDS AT THE PEAK OF GTP

After failing to win Daytona the year before with two Group C versions of the R90C prototypes entered by the NPTI team, Nissan was not to be denied in 1992. Four cars were entered: two factory-backed R91CKs from Japan fielded by Nissan Motorsports (NISMO) and two R90Cs fielded by the NPTI crew. Running in the Group C class, which meant no Camel GT points, Japan's Masahiro Hasemi, Kazuyoshi Hoshino, and Toshio Suzuki won overall following an eight-hour battle with the NPTI team.

The season opener introduced a new marquee sponsorship for the Daytona endurance classic. The prestigious brand Rolex replaced SunBank as the title sponsor of the twenty-four-hour event, launching one of racing's most famous traditions. All the class-winning drivers earned a coveted Rolex Daytona watch engraved with their names.

The impressive performance by the Japanese drivers and crews at Daytona helped open a new chapter in the international presence of IMSA. In addition to engaging Group C cars under an equivalence formula at the newly named Rolex 24 at Daytona, there were other landmark international forays. IMSA made the first of three year-end trips to Japan at the end of the 1992 season. Several officials, GT cars, and teams were invited by race organizer Road Runners Club in conjunction with the Japan Automobile Federation (JAF), which was looking to start a national GT series. In December 1992, IMSA began international involvement closer to home by supporting an FIA effort initiated by its president Max Mosley to strengthen the GT championship sponsored by Marlboro in the Caribbean region.

In addition to the contingent from Japan, the race entry included a Group C Porsche-powered Courage, which unfortunately fell out of the race in unusual fashion in one of the worst crashes in the race's history. Occasioned by a blown tire due

The GT traffic at Turn One of Daytona gets crowded. *Brian Cleary*

to high downforce on the track's banking, the incident became a precursor to other big crashes over the course of the GTP season.

In the early morning darkness around 3 a.m., Pascal Fabre was at the wheel when the Courage blew a right-rear tire heading into the tri-oval at 200 miles per hour. The failed tire disintegrated the rear bodywork, which upset the aerodynamics, flipped the car, and sent it airborne. The flying car narrowly passed underneath the starter's stand, which at that time hung out over the track at the start/finish line, missing it by inches. The Courage then careened into the fencing near Turn One, shedding its engine, gearbox, all four wheels, and various parts before the bare chassis and tub came to rest upside down at the point formed by the grass that separated Pit Lane from the track.

The helpless driver was left hanging upside down in his harness while fuel spilled from the remains of the chassis. Within seconds, the Japanese NISMO crew members, who were pitted in the last stall, ran across Pit Road to the rescue. They got to the remains of the car just in time to roll the chassis over—nearly on top of the driver who was doing his best to get out of it! One IMSA staff member stationed at the end of Pit Road went with the Japanese crew to organize the international chaos into a proper rescue operation. (The French driver spoke very little English. Neither he nor the IMSA official spoke Japanese.)

When the track rescue vehicles arrived seconds later, the driver was out of the remains of the car, which was right side up and sitting in a large puddle of fuel. Parts and debris were scattered from the start/finish line through Turn One. The impact sheared five sections of fence posts off the concrete wall on the front straight. Debris, fencing, and cables were ripped out and scattered down the track and into the grandstands, where thankfully there were no fans during the wee hours. Nobody was seriously injured, but it sure scared a lot of folks into being careful with suspension camber

The factory NISMO team entered its R91CK in the Le Mans class at Daytona and outran the field. *Peter Gloede*

NISSAN
NISMO
ICHIKOH
23
ICHIKOH
NISSAN
GOODYEAR

The leading R91CK during a pit stop on Sunday. The NISMO team competed under Group C rules. *Rick Dole*

and tire pressure settings. After almost two hours of caution to repair the fencing mounted on top of the concrete wall, the race resumed. Later, a complete redesign of the starter stand occurred, and it no longer hung out over the track.

The next major endurance event proved pivotal for Nissan. Leading the 12 Hours at Sebring in the final hours after sunset, the Nissan NPT-91 faltered with an electrical issue and made a pit stop to restore functioning headlights, losing five laps and a shot at Victory Lane.

At the time, there was no supplemental lighting for TV at Sebring. Without powerful lights on the cars, navigating the track proved challenging even

With a team managed by Gary Cummings, the Porsche 962 of Vern Schuppan claimed third at the Rolex 24 and second in GTP. *Brian Cleary*

The winning Nissan prototype slowed at the finish to be joined by the GTS-class Nissan 300ZX Turbo of Clayton Cunningham Racing, enabling others to join in. *NASCAR Archives and Research Center*

at slow speeds. Sometimes, an alternator or battery failure at the wrong place made it nearly impossible to return to the pits. It was so dark that drivers like Brabham confessed that after spinning they had to wait for a car to go past before knowing where to rejoin. Circumstances had not changed much from the race's early days when drivers sometimes drove off the end of the World War II–era airport's main runway after missing the turn to the back-straight.

The Eagle Toyota of All American Racers stormed past the Nissan into the lead and was not challenged for the remainder of the twelve-hour race. The balance of power in the Camel GT shifted in the span of a few laps from Nissan to Toyota, and from that point forward it was almost all Toyotas in Victory Lane in 1992 and 1993.

Nissan, Toyota, and Jaguar continued to share one problem—high-speed crashes. At Road Atlanta, Nissan suffered two catastrophic tire failures in the dip prior to the bridge where speeds were well over 200 mph, resulting in the cars of Brabham and Robinson going end over end several times. Brabham was uninjured, but Robinson spent a few days recuperating in the hospital following his accident. Fangio had an equally frightening incident, but he managed to keep the car upright and crawl back to Pit Lane despite a missing rear corner that was torn off when a tire exploded in the dip.

The tire/suspension loading was becoming difficult to manage at several tracks as the high speeds and the amazing amount of aero downforce being created tortured the components. With massive amounts of power and torque, this generation of GTP cars were some of the fastest road racing cars ever built. Rear springs of 7,200 to 8,000 pounds were not uncommon on the top cars. Running more than 7,000 pounds of downforce—despite engines restricted to 800 horsepower—on top of the car's mechanical grip required supermen to drive them. Lateral g-forces, acceleration, and braking were all dramatically enhanced by the latest developments.

Tube-frame cars with diverse engines fostered close competition and contributed to the ongoing success of IMSA's GT class. *Lee Self*

NISSAN
Cunningham
RACING
Snap-on

Juan Manuel Fangio II focusing on the job at hand—winning the Camel GT championship in the Toyota Eagle MKIII. *Peter Gloede*

The physical aspect of keeping a car under control was becoming more and more challenging.

According to urban myth, the GTP cars generated so much downforce that one could run upside down on the bottom of a highway bridge if the car's speed was more than 165 mph—in theory! But to the best of everyone's knowledge, no one ever tried it.

Jaguar countered Toyota with a new XJR-14 powered by the 3.5-liter Cosworth V8 that was derived from the Formula One engine that had been raced in the TWR team's Group C entries. At Lime Rock, while leading the race after twenty laps, the left rear of the Jaguar failed on the flat-out last corner leading onto the front straight, resulting in a big crash. At the time, little Lime Rock had one

Dan Gurney and his All American Racers (AAR) started in GTU with Toyota Celicas before moving to GTO with a turbo version. The all-conquering Eagle MKIII was the third prototype developed by AAR. *Peter Gloede*

Scott Schubot's Buick-Spice won numerous Camel Light races and a championship. *Peter Gloede*

of the fastest average lap speeds in the championship. Reportedly, the fastest GTP cars went flat out from the top of the hill on the far side of the course, under the bridge, and through the last corner's apex at around 130 mph. They continued flat out down the front straight, passing the pit exit at around 170 mph before gathering it all up for braking into Turn One. On a 1.7-mile-long track . . .

Following the installation of the backstraight "bus stop" chicane at Watkins Glen after the accident of Tommy Kendall in the Intrepid and the fatal crash of J. D. McDuffie in NASCAR's Cup Series in 1991, Jones would stun all those who thought the course adjustment would slow ground effect cars. He qualified his Jaguar on the short course pole at an average speed of over 150 mph, which remains the single fastest official qualifying lap on a road course in North American motorsport history.

What in fact occurred was a change in the braking for the GTP cars on the short course regularly used by NASCAR. There was no longer full braking at the end of the backstraight and instead slight

CompTech's version of an Acura-powered Spice became the dominant force in the final two years of Camel Light competition. *Peter Gloede*

After resolving fires from overheated exhausts, the RX-792P showed promise. The Mazda GTP program ended before the car could be developed into a winner. *Peter Gloede*

braking before the bus stop after coming flat out through Turn One, Turn Two, and the esses. Drivers then powered through the chicane at speed, around the big turnaround corner at the end of the straight, and all the way back to the next-to-last lefthand turn, still at full throttle. Essentially, the only braking was going into Turn One and the last two turns. The rest of the lap was full throttle everywhere. So much for a bus stop to slow them down.

The lightweight Jag, always fast but fragile on the rough American circuits, limited Jones to a pair of victories after taking the top GTP points at Daytona in an XJR-12. P. J. Jones won two races in a MKIII for Toyota, Brabham captured one victory, and Fangio scored six more victories after Sebring en route to the championship. He would take home a record total of purse, point fund, and Camel bonus money of over $570,000 for a season's work in sports car racing.

Mazda debuted its four-rotor GTP RX-792P prototype and scored several top finishes with Cobb and Halsmer as the primary drivers. Mazda had already established a strong program in Group C and was capitalizing on its Le Mans victory in

Chip Robinson became Geoff Brabham's teammate at NPTI, resulting in some intense competition for race victories. *Peter Gloede*

The Nissan NPT-90 GTP's aerodynamic demonstration in wet conditions. *Lee Self*

1991 with a four-rotor Group C car by bringing the technology and the engine's sound to the US market. Early thermal management issues around the four-rotor exhaust temperature (rumored to be over 1,700 degrees) melted parts of the chassis and were responsible for several engine bay fires before the heat problem was sorted out.

Moretti and Oscar Larrauri carried the flag for the Joest Porsche 962C fans and scored numerous top finishes with Larrauri ending up fifth in the championship. David Tennyson, Kendall, and Taylor delivered top performances in Chevrolet-powered Spices and Intrepids but took home no winner trophies.

After dominating and winning the Lights championship in 1991, Parker Johnstone, the CompTech team, and Acura once again took overall honors. Johnstone won seven races—six with regular

co-driver Dan Marvin and one with Melgrati, who added two more victories co-driving with Taylor and Costas Los. Developed by CompTech and installed in a Spice chassis, the Acura NSX V6 was proving to be a potent and reliable rival to the Mazda rotary, Buick V6, and Ferrari V8 engines that had been the basis of the category.

Out of thirteen Lights races, Mazda took one win at Sebring, where Downing's twin rotor Mazda-Kudzu was co-driven with Tim McAdam. Buick scored five victories shared between the Buick-Kudzus of Scandia Motorsport that were driven by team owner Evans with Fermín Vélez and by Tommy Riggins and Charles Morgan.

## FUEL CRISIS

By Mark Raffauf

Rules around turbo restricitons were imposed by IMSA to control the performance of turbo engines versus normally aspirated powerplants. By 1992, the continued advancement of turbocharging technology and engine management meant that fuel was becoming a major element in loosening up many of those restrictions.

The only event that required all participants to run the same fuel was the Rolex 24 at Daytona, where Union 76 had been the supplier for decades. This single source requirement eliminated many of the logistical, storage, and safety concerns around the large quantity of fuel that was required for the race.

Teams brought their own fuel to all other events. The IMSA Code of Regulations published fuel specifications to ensure that team fuel would be comparable to the high-quality Union 76 race gas used at Daytona.

However, it became clear something was going on. More and more fuel handlers were using gas masks while working with these fuels, and horsepower levels remained constant and did not appear to be "restricted" by the intake restrictors required in the rulebook.

At Watkins Glen, IMSA took samples from three top GTP teams for its own information and with no intention of enforcing anything from these preliminary tests. Exxon, IMSA's new series partner, graciously had its labs test the fuel with a clear understanding that the company would not in any way be involved with any rule enforcement process. The results were not unexpected. Two samples were close to the IMSA specification, one was not.

The next event was Road America, and IMSA took five samples from GTP teams' fuel rigs during the race—one each from Nissan, Mazda, and Joest's Porsche 962C and two from Toyota's GTP cars. The samples were labeled A, B, C, D, and E and forwarded to Core Laboratories in Houston, a laboratory certified by the American Society for Testing and Materials (ASTM).

The Road America race results remained provisional until Core returned its results from the fuel samples in late August. IMSA was aware of what to expect through daily contact with Core. It was not a witch hunt, and we did not like the potential of such ramifications. After receiving the results, points were not awarded to four of the five cars due to their fuel not meeting ASTM D439-89 specifications. The exception was Reinhold Joest's Porsche 962 entry.

Those who lost their points appealed the decision based on how the samples were taken, maintained,

## TRANS-AM TEAMS JOIN GTS

The GT programs continued to flourish and grow in a year when the Olivetti-sponsored Rocketsports team of Paul Gentilozzi, Les Lindley, and a number of other past Trans-Am series competitors joined the Exxon Supreme Series circus. Some of the transfers then went on to win.

The new GTS designation was introduced for the more powerful class leaders while the traditional GTO designation was given to the competitors running under the All-American Challenge rules for V8 entries.

A season-long GTS battle erupted between the Clayton Cunningham–prepared Nissan 300ZX Turbos of Steve Millen and Jeremy Dale and the Oldsmobile Cutlasses of Rocketsports drivers Paul Gentilozzi and Darin Brassfield. Roush returned for three events in 1992 with Whistler-sponsored Mustangs and won the Rolex 24 once again with Gordon, Wally Dallenbach Jr., and Schroeder.

and shipped, and IMSA quickly realized how complicated future attempts at fuel monitoring would be. It was beyond IMSA's capabilities and resources at that time to enforce the required specification. Points were reinstated and everyone accepted the circumstances and moved on. For IMSA, moving on meant working with Exxon to produce the first unleaded racing gasoline, which would be required for use by all competitors at all events for the 1994 season. Game over.

It should be noted that the argument over process revolved around the temperature of the fuel sample in the field compared with laboratory testing temperature and the impact this change could have on the test results. The samples taken at Watkins Glen at one temperature were in fact almost identical to those taken at Road America at a different temperature. This indicated the variable temperature of the two samples, tested by two separate qualified laboratories, did not have a significant impact on the test results. High concentrations of anti-knock chemicals were found in the fuel. (Anti-knock chemicals inhibit preignition in an internal combustion engine—such as lead—and are an integral part of petroleum products like gasoline.) The fuel in the two Toyotas measured 81.96 percent toluene, which was unaffected by temperature changes. Toluene soon became the initial replacement for lead in all automotive gasolines until it was found to be even more toxic than the lead it was replacing. Toluene could bring significant health problems with prolonged exposure.

The use of these chemicals was not prohibited in the regulations so long as the fuel met the required ASTM specification. The anti-knock (pre-detonation) characteristics of these types of chemicals allowed significantly higher boost pressures to be used and subsequently produced more power.

These types of fuels were developed in the mid-to-late 1980s for the 1.5-liter Formula One engines. Eventually, they were used to allegedly produce (along with other tricky stuff) up to one horsepower per cubic centimeter of displacement, which meant 1,500 horsepower for a 1.5-liter engine for brief periods of time in qualifying. Of course, after energy production at that level there was not much left of the engine for anything else, and a new engine was required, one that was raced at much lower levels of boost.

In the end, IMSA backed away from a protracted legal and technical battle that would not have done anything positive for the sport and accepted the fact that the processes needed to enforce the regulations were beyond the practical means that were available in the short-term. The future of racing would require a spec fuel to be used by everyone in the same manner. Exxon was coming.

Gordon returned to Portland for a fourth-place finish and then won the finale in Del Mar.

With four victories, Millen captured the championship by four points over Gentilozzi, who won two races. Irv Hoerr scored the GTO title in a Rocketsports Cutlass over Lindley's Camaro and Joe Llauget's Cutlass in the nine-race sprint championship run in conjunction with the GTS cars. In GTU, the drivers of the Leitzinger team's Nissan 240SXs finished one-two in the championship with the super-quick David Loring winning the title over Butch Leitzinger, who was just beginning his long and successful career. Butch's father Bob finished third in the championship to give Nissan drivers a sweep of the podium. John Fergus and Don Walker earned four wins in the Infinity Car Audio-liveried Dodge Daytonas.

In yet another Rolex 24 at Daytona win for the Mazda RX-7, Dick Greer, Al Bacon, Peter Uria, and Mike Mees were the victors. The Oldsmobile

Motorsports Achieva joined the GTU chase at the twenty-four-hour race and began to show promise before departing for further development.

Foretelling the future and emphasizing the strong ties to Latin America that IMSA had fostered over the years, 25 percent of the grid in GTS/GTO and GTU race at the Miami Grand Prix was from the Caribbean basin, Central America, and South America. Drivers and teams from the Dominican Republic, Puerto Rico, Haiti, Panama, Peru, and Ecuador enjoyed the opportunity to race in South Florida. They regularly competed in the FIA-sanctioned region known as NACAM. (In addition to references to North and Central America, the acronym included a reference to Mexico, although it is technically part of North America.)

The four IMSA-supported series continued in 1992, with one difference. The International

The Applebee's-backed Oldsmobile-Spice entered by Tom Milner regularly finished in the top five and on the podium.
*Peter Gloede*

Sedan Series sponsorship shifted to *Automobile Magazine*. Otherwise, the consistency and stability of the different series continued to provide solid opportunities for competitors. The Firestone Firehawk and Bridgestone Supercar series increased entries and gained notoriety, although newer model Firehawk cars were increasingly more complicated, expensive, and difficult to prepare. These developments also made rule enforcement a bigger challenge for IMSA's technical staff., and without manufacturer support, they were becoming impractical to run.

The spec series known at the time as the Barber Saab Pro Series once again promoted close open-wheel competition and an upwardly mobile cast of young drivers. Created in 1986 by CEO of Saab USA Bob Sinclair, Skip Barber, and IMSA founder Bishop, it was a national series of professional events that showcased the top level of the rapidly growing Barber's Driving School ladder system. It provided IMSA with good-looking open-wheel cars and a series featuring close competition. A significant number of drivers took the opportunity to advance within the sport after a season in Barber Saab as well as Barber's Driving School.

Indy 500 winner Danny Sullivan, a Barber's Driving School graduate, presented Robert Amren with the championship trophy and a $100,000 career-enhancement check to help pay for future racing endeavors at the season-ending awards ceremony. P. J. Jones and Ashton Lewis challenged Amren all year, but they came up short due to a few missed races on Jones's part and a couple of DNFs and lower finishes by Lewis. The series helped facilitate the rapid advancement of young Jones, who would return to IMSA in 1993 as the second driver in the Eagle MKIIIs as a teammate to Fangio.

Inside IMSA, the efforts of the sanctioning body and participants meant momentum had been sustained despite difficulties with new ownership and sponsor changes. The packaging of three live NBC telecasts of races combined with *USA Today* newspaper supplement sections played an important role in sustaining momentum. At a time where it was not thought to be a good idea to invest in promotion, due to a shrinking economy in the aftermath of the Gulf War, major advertising came from the car companies participating in GTP and GT, tire and beer companies, and the Camel brand, which was eligible to participate in print advertising.

Mike Huling deserved a lot of the credit for coordinating the projects and for making sure they did not become major economic hemorrhages for IMSA. IMSA did not want to be in the business of putting together TV packages due to their required financing. Over time its racing became sufficiently attractive to various networks for them to pay rights fees for programming in the 1980s. The first live ESPN coverage of an auto race was one of IMSA's Kelly American Challenge races at Lime Rock—up the road from ESPN's original headquarters in Bristol, Connecticut. As the TV world expanded with cable, more networks came online, and many sports organizations started looking to be on TV. Expectations from the networks got higher, and Huling did a good job of managing those expectations.

Despite the outward trappings of success, the staff at IMSA that Dan Greenwood led felt the pressure of obvious warnings about the future. Between Greenwood, Bishop, Cooper, and staff members Mark Raffauf and George Silbermann, a realistic view of what needed to be done for the future was gradually established with owner Cone. A lot of issues needed to be addressed. The sponsorship from the Camel brand was scheduled to end. Entries in GTP were dwindling. The FIA's World Sports Car Championship—the final offshoot of Group C—was failing rapidly, and it was likely some of the existing IMSA participants would limit or halt their future activities due to the economy.

# THE INTERNATIONAL IN IMSA

By Mark Raffauf

During the waning days of the GTP and Group C prototypes in the early 1990s, the popularity of IMSA GT racing began to soar. Powerful, fire-breathing cars from Nissan, Ford, Ferrari, Oldsmobile, Chevrolet, and Mazda were a big hit in the US and were attracting attention from the rest of the world. In a break from road racing tradition, the IMSA GT cars were being built from the ground up as tube frame chassis instead of being derived from an actual production car. The cars had flat bottoms that cut down significantly on the cost for aero testing, which was part of the high expense of competing with prototypes. This made it relatively easy for manufacturers and private entrants to build and source reasonably priced hardware that would put them at the front of the GT field.

The advent of this new era of IMSA GT cars eventually led to a new chapter in the ongoing alliance with the Japan Automobile Federation (JAF). Throughout the 1980s, IMSA founder Bishop and officials at the JAF built a healthy friendship. Both organizations sanctioned domestic prototype programs of their own making that were independent from the FIA, and both held similar political positions when it came to world motorsports.

For three consecutive years in the early 1990s, a race was held in Japan between invited IMSA teams and Japanese entries. These race meetings became the foundation for the JAF to build its highly successful GT racing series, which would eventually replace the All Japan Sports Prototype Championship and became yet another significant chapter of IMSA's international presence.

## IMSA's International History

The "International" in the IMSA name first came to fruition when the Camel GT's next-to-last round was held at the Autódromo Hermanos Rodriguez in Mexico City in 1974. An all-Mexican driving lineup of Guillermo Rojas, Héctor Rebaque, and Freddy van Beuren won the 1000 Kilometers of Mexico City in a Porsche RSR over twenty-one regular IMSA teams and nineteen Mexican/Central American teams. The race opened the door for Mexican, Central American, and Caribbean racers to compete over the course of the full IMSA schedule for decades to come.

A year later, IMSA ventured north of the US border to the Mosport Park circuit east of Toronto for the first of many Canadian events. Already flush with some of Canada's top sports car racers participating, the first Mosport event began an ongoing tradition of IMSA racing in Canada.

By the mid-1970s, IMSA's prominence in the world fostered the IMSA class at the famed 24 Hours of Le Mans, specifically created to attract US-based teams, drivers, and their unique IMSA All American Grand Touring (AAGT) tube frame cars, such as John Greenwood Corvettes, DeKon Monzas, and NASCAR International Stock Cars. Drivers and teams from IMSA began populating the Le Mans entry list year after year, which became another ongoing tradition. The American cars evolved over the years, but they were always fan favorites, especially those with big American V8 engines.

As time went on, the logistics of moving full-blown teams and trucks to Europe for an event that fell in the middle of the Camel GT schedule grew more challenging. Many drivers made the trip on their own and participated with European-based cars and teams. The Whittington brothers won at Le Mans in 1979 in the first Kremer Racing Porsche 935 K3, which they purchased and brought back to race in IMSA a week later.

In the late 1970s, the FIA created the World Endurance Championship by linking a series of worldwide events in Europe, the US, Central America, and Asia that allowed drivers to score points in a variety of events and cars. Each race contributed $10,000 to a point fund that was divided at the conclusion of the season according to points earned by the top drivers. The first champions were John Paul Sr., who was followed a year later by Bob Garretson. Both were IMSA regulars in the Camel GT.

'93 JSS SERIES '93 3/27、28

(JAPAN SUPER SPORTS SEDAN RACE)

The new All Japan GT Car Championship was touted along with the IMSA GT cars for the race at Fuji in March 1993.
*Mark Raffauf*

## RACING IN JAPAN

For three consecutive years beginning in 1992, IMSA and GT participants headed to the Far East at the invitation of Japan's Road Runners Club (RRC). The RRC race organizers were known for introducing NHRA drag racing to the country by inviting alcohol Funny Cars, dragsters, and drag bikes to race on Fuji Speedway's long front straight. The RRC took a visionary role in supporting GT racing as the future of Japan's premier road racing series.

When it came to prototypes and GT series, Japan and the US were experiencing a similar dynamic. The All Japan Sports Prototype Championship had been very successful under the Group C rules along with its cousin in the US, the Camel GTP. But the JSPC began winding down once the newly introduced and disastrous 3.5-liter engine formula hastened Group C's downfall in the early 1990s. The demise of the Group C class run by the FIA was thanks to this new engine configuration that failed to gain support from manufacturers or fans. This meant the Japanese could no longer rely on Group C cars or participants to sustain its national championship. The possibility

The majestic Mount Fuji vanished behind a wall of rain when IMSA's GT cars ran their first event at the Fuji International Raceway. *Mark Raffauf*

A combined IMSA and Japanese GT field raced at Autopolis in 1994. *IMSA Archive*

of using GT cars to build a new national championship then became the focus of the JAF.

In addition to the Nissan Skylines that were based on the road car that had been homologated for Group A, the beginnings of the Japanese GT Championship already had some RX-7s and Nissan Silvias, (known as the 240SX in the US) that provided solid competition to the IMSA teams and drivers.

In November 1992, under the shadow of the great Mount Fuji, an early snow canceled IMSA's test day. Drivers spent hours at the hotel practicing on two new Sony Formula One video game machines that featured the Fuji circuit. Things were going well until the crews figured out that by tilting the machines dramatically, they could recreate the potential g-loads of the corners. When driver Jeremy Dale was inadvertently pitched out of the seat onto the floor, the hotel manager promptly threw everyone out of the game room for the duration of the visit.

The first Fuji race was a bit of a mismatch since the Japanese teams and cars were not yet comparable to the more powerful IMSA GTS cars, such as the Nissan 300ZX Twin Turbos entered by Cunningham's team, a Roush Racing Ford Mustang, and a V8 from the ranks of All American GT teams. In GTU, the Japanese and Americans were better balanced

Judged too treacherous, the original high-banked Turn One was dropped from the Fuji circuit soon after it opened.
*Bruce Clarke*

The IMSA cars took a train ride in containers across the US before being sailed across the Pacific and eventually landing in Japan. *Bruce Clarke*

Car owner Bob Leitzinger (right) and driver/crew chief Carson Baird (hand on car) show their Nissan 240SX to Japanese officials and team principals. *Bruce Clarke*

Clayton Cunningham's GTS-class 300ZX built to silhouette rules sitting next to a road-going version of the Nissan. The Japanese quickly identified with the IMSA concept. *Mark Raffauf Collection*

Bill Auberlen's RX-7 would win the GTU class and finish third overall behind two Skylines during a heavy downpour in the 1992 race for IMSA and Japanese GT teams. *Mark Raffauf Collection*

Les Lindley's immaculate Mustang GTO car was significantly damaged when it was rear-ended by a Nissan Skyline at speed on the front straight in the heavy rain. *Mark Raffauf*

The Nissan IMSA GTS and GTU cars weathered a classic Fuji deluge during the inaugural trip to Japan. *Mark Raffauf Collection*

because both had Nissans and Mazdas that were more comparable in horsepower. Millen won in the Cunningham Nissan by a lap over one of the Skyline drivers, and Bob Leitzinger's Nissan 240SX took honors in GTU.

The second event at Fuji the following year awarded full points to Japanese teams and competitors in the inaugural 1993 All Japan Grand Touring Car Championship race. Much had changed because the Japanese had used the IMSA entries from the previous year as benchmarks. For example, the first of the new all-wheel-drive Nissan Skyline GT-Rs built by factory team NISMO were installed with additional turbocharging to their inline six-cylinder engines, bringing their horsepower closer to the more than 600 horsepower employed by the American 300ZX.

The entry also featured several of the older Skylines racing against cars from the AAGT that were representing the Americans in the GTS category. IMSA's contingent was made up of Riggins and Joe Lauget driving Oldsmobile Cutlasses and Lindley in his Ford Mustang. In GTU, Japanese RX-7s and a NISMO Silvia raced against Bill Auberlen in an RX-7,

Veteran IMSA driver and crew chief Carson Baird surveys the GTU competition on a rainy race day. *Mark Raffauf*

Numerous Japanese competitors entered makes and models that were not sold in the US or intended to be race cars.
*Mark Raffauf*

Bob Leitzinger and Frank Honsowetz in Leitzinger's Nissan 240SXs, and Jack Lewis in a Porsche 911.

The twenty-five-car grid was hampered on race day by the notorious Fuji rain, which poured down all day. In Japan you race regardless. Riggins and Lindley were both involved in accidents, with Lindley's being the most dramatic. He slowed down on the one-mile front straight, because he could not see, and got rear-ended by a Skyline going almost full speed. By that point the all-wheel-drive GT-R Skylines had already pulled away and were gone. Finishing third overall, Auberlen technically won his first career IMSA race by beating all the entries in his GTU class and all but two of the eight Skylines in the field during the torrential downpour.

The event had a significant result beyond the dominance of the single new NISMO Skyline GT-R. JAF President Kazuo Suzuki, a longtime fan and friend of IMSA, convened a round table meeting with all the Japanese manufacturers to review the IMSA entries. Representatives of Japanese manufacturers asked questions of their US counterparts and IMSA officials. The Japanese were totally intrigued with the cars' performance, robust construction, exotic but clearly recognizable silhouette style bodywork, and the ease of maintenance and repair.

What fascinated the Japanese the most—manufacturers, teams, and fans—were the headlight decals used by IMSA teams instead of actual headlights. Many wanted to walk up and touch them, because by then IMSA's teams had mastered creating headlight covers that from six feet away could hardly be differentiated from the real thing. The fans were polite about not touching anything until the IMSA teams began inviting them into the garages, which apparently was also a new experience for our newfound Japanese friends.

JAF continued to focus on building its All Japan Grand Touring Car Championship, which became Super GT in 2005. The Japanese were experts in understanding the concept of real race cars and the innovation that could be applied to them when built as tube frame silhouette vehicles. They took the idea and ran with it according to their goals. The long-run-

The factory Nismo Nissan GTS Skyline (No. 2) and GTU Silvia, known as a 240SX in the US, were strong contenders.
*Mark Raffauf*

Nestled within an extinct volcanic crater, the Autopolis circuit on the south island of Kyushu hosted the final race with IMSA teams. *Mark Raffauf*

Jim Pace drove Eduardo Dibos's RX-7, which touted the car owner's native Peru to the Japanese. *Mark Raffauf*

Autopolis was one of the most modern circuits in the world at the time, with beautiful infrastructure, buildings, garages, and a five-star hotel. *Mark Raffauf*

Frequently encountering beer vending machines was one of the cultural experiences IMSA visitors enjoyed. *Mark Raffauf Collection*

ning Super GT remains one of the most popular and successful racing formulas in the world, and it was created at the national level and not by the FIA. Super GT further helped accelerate a street tuner cult that flourished worldwide, including the US.

The third race was held the following year at the ultramodern Autopolis circuit on the island of Kyushu. Spectacularly set in an extinct volcanic caldera, it was beautiful and new—but an unfortunately long way from anywhere or anything. All the race participants stayed in the five-star hotel on the outside of Turn One, and all three meals were served in the track cafeteria. Getting to and from this exotic racetrack location was an adventure. The Americans learned that commuter flights from Tokyo to the southernmost island of Kyushu were made on board a Boeing 747!

IMSA entries, including Cunningham's 300ZX Twin Turbos, demonstrated their full capacities in the dry conditions at Autopolis. The two American-built

The entire IMSA contingent in Pit Lane. Noticeable individuals include Berdie Martin, president of ACCUS, and Anne Martin; Mr. Nakajima and Mr. Murikami, hosts for the Road Runners Club; drivers Steve Millen, Johnny O'Connell, Bill Auberlen, Charles Morgan, Jim Pace, Bob and Butch Leitzinger, and Tommy Riggins; and IMSA's George Silbermann, Don Schnieders, and Christine Raffauf. *Mark Raffauf Collection*

Nissans put on a clinic, racing among themselves far out front in a contest that Johnny O'Connell won by seven seconds over Millen. Unfortunately, because it was an exhibition event and not part of the championship, the Japanese entry featured no Skylines and had only five cars.

The teams and officials took time to tour while in Japan. They visited the world-famous Tokyo Tsukiji Market at 3:00 a.m. to watch the daily auctions in the world's largest and cleanest fish market, which covers several city blocks. A fully restored samurai castle, local grocery stores, and towns that rarely saw foreigners were among the highlights of the tours. The people in Japan were wonderful, and many of the participants left there after one or more events with a newfound respect for the Japanese people, culture, lifestyle, and food. Butch Leitzinger had his name painted on his helmet in Japanese kanji. He kept it on his helmet for the rest of his racing career, proud to have been part of IMSA GT going worldwide.

TOYOTA
99
TOYOTA
98
NISSAN
30
momo
RODIO
BOSCH
Castrol
2
JAGUAR
32
EXXON
Wynn's
20
16
6
FAT
BOSCH

CHAPTER FOUR

# 1993: GTP CHAPTER COMES TO A CLOSE

A lot had changed by the twenty-fifth anniversary of IMSA. The sanctioning body had started in 1969 with small open-wheel Formula Fords on ovals and road courses, and by 1993 the GTP prototypes were competing at 200 miles per hour on the greatest road racing circuits in North America. One of the longest running motorsports sponsorships had been instrumental to this growth. But this, too, was about to change. The backing of the Camel GT would end after twenty years due to government-imposed restrictions on tobacco advertising and marketing. A great chapter of motorsports history created under the Camel brand banner was about to close.

Toyota's championship winner Juan Manuel Fangio II and teammate P. J. Jones, who was the runner-up, dominated the final Camel GT season. Jones, the son of racing legend Parnelli Jones, won three of the duo's titanic battles during the season, including the Rolex 24 at Daytona. But starting at the season's second race in Miami, Fangio was brilliant and was driving much like his namesake uncle by winning six straight events. IMSA made efforts to use air restrictors to reduce the power of the potent Toyotas of All American Racers. Team owner Dan Gurney said the sanctioning body was trying to make his engines breathe "through a hummingbird's asshole." Nevertheless, the team's Eagle MKIII dominated the season.

With team owner Gurney letting them race, Fangio and Jones fought like rivals. They were often only separated by seconds and relied on pit work and strategy to determine the outcome between them.

At Daytona, the two Toyotas swapped the lead eight times over the first 257 laps before Fangio's No. 99 stumbled and eventually retired. The TWR team's Bud Light XJR-12D assumed the chase of the

The competition between Juan Manuel Fangio II and P. J. Jones in their Eagle MKIIIs was fierce throughout the season. *NASCAR Archive and Research Center*

remaining Toyota, and the two teams swapped the lead for much of the rest of the race. Three Walkinshaw Jaguars were entered in IMSA's Le Mans class, which meant they were still eligible for championship points as stated in the regulations, but two had retired early. The remaining Jaguar of Davy Jones, Scott Pruett, and Scott Goodyear kept up the chase into Sunday afternoon until its engine expired.

When the Toyota of Jones, Mark Dismore, and Rocky Moran was slowed by gearbox problems that required a long pit stop on Pit Road for repairs, the No. 30 MOMO Nissan NPT-90 driven by car owner Moretti, Derek Bell, John Paul Jr., and Massimo Sigala was vaulted into a comfortable lead. The team and car looked sure to post the first victory in the Rolex by Moretti, who was in his fifteenth year of trying. But with ninety minutes to go, the engine expired, another victim of the torrid pace established by the Toyota turbos. The No. 98 Eagle inherited the win by simply surviving, the high-revving 2.1-liter, four-cylinder turbo bringing Toyota and AAR their biggest endurance race victory.

At the sprint race in Miami, the Toyotas dominated, taking first and second only four seconds apart. Notable was David Tennyson's stellar third place drive with Price Cobb in a 7.2-liter Chevy-Spice. Moretti and Bell claimed fourth in the

By early Sunday morning, the No. 98 Eagle had suffered ongoing mechanical problems and did not look like a Rolex 24 winner. *Lee Self*

Campaigning a Nissan NPT-90 in 1993, Moretti's MOMO team would have to wait five years before scoring a twenty-four-hour victory at Daytona. *Peter Gloede*

MOMO Nissan, beginning a season-long run to points-paying positions.

A rainy race day at Sebring made it challenging for all, and another close call erupted between Toyota and Nissan. Paul Jr., at the wheel of the MOMO Nissan, ran down Jones for second and was closing in on the leading Toyota of Fangio and Wallace in the darkness before time ran out. Fangio and Wallace became the first drivers to win Sebring back-to-back.

Paul Jr. was always a threat to win in whatever car he drove, and on any given day he could outdrive everybody on the track. Victory Lane would elude him for a while, but it was not long until he was back on the top step in sports cars and Indy cars.

The second sprint race of the year was held at the Atlanta Motor Speedway, located south of the city, and not at the traditional Road Atlanta circuit on the north side of town. The oval/road course combination turned out to be a spectacular circuit for watching GTP cars, because they could be followed for a full lap—even by those standing on Pit Road. The high-speed high banks and a tricky infield offered a more intimate view of the sights and sounds of road racing than the bigger track at Daytona but with the same exhilarating speed. The two Toyotas battling side by side on the banking for almost the entire race was a breathtaking forerunner of a season where the teammates would go back and forth.

The West Coast events were won by the narrowest of margins. Fangio prevailed at Portland by only a second over Jones, and at the season finale in Phoenix a race-long fight was decided by a single pit stop.

Reinhold Joest campaigned two of his latest development Porsche 962Cs for Manuel Reuter, Paul Jr., and John Winter. The German team scored

Repairs made in a safe place were allowed during the Rolex 24. Near a port-a-john was a safe place! *NASCAR Archive and Research Center*

Back in the day, standing by the fence at Daytona was still OK. *NASCAR Archive and Research Center*

one win at Road America, the last major sports car race victory for a Porsche 962 and the end of the 962's amazing ten-year run and winning career.

Over the course of the season, MOMO men Moretti, Bell, and occasionally Paul Jr. made a valiant effort with the season-long Nissan NPT-90 customer program that followed the departure of Nissan's NPTI team. But they came up short several times and could only score podium finishes behind the Toyotas.

Tennyson, usually driving with Cobb, ran a Spice with big Chevy V8 power that was near or at the front for much of the season. Taylor campaigned one of the Chevrolet Intrepid GTP cars that was left over from the Pratt & Miller efforts of the previous two years. Under the direction of Michael Gue, the cars were always fast but suffered from the mandatory use of iron brakes in place of carbon and were sometimes plagued by reliability issues. Along with Famous

Amos Cookies, Taylor's program put new sponsor Danka on the car for the first time. That began a long and fruitful relationship between Taylor and the company, which produced better marketing results off the track than race finishes in its first year.

Fangio II claimed his second consecutive championship in the final season of the Camel GTP. *Lee Self*

In Camel Lights, Parker Johnstone was dominant overall with six wins in the CompTech Acura-Spice, although the Brix Racing version of the same car with Bob Schader and Bob Earl earned four wins.

In its three seasons, CompTech's Acuras won three championships, twenty-two Camel Lights races, and only failed to finish in the top five seven times.

Jim Downing's Mazda-Kudzu, shared with regular co-drivers Tim McAdam, John Grooms, and Frank Jellinek Jr., won at Daytona in typical Mazda fashion with good speed and phenomenal reliability. They would record steady podium finishes during most of the eleven-race season to score a third place in the final Lights championship. Downing helped create the entire Lights concept nine years earlier and won the first three championships. Through the final Lights season in 1993, he was not only a participant, but a car and engine provider to the category.

The Lights race at Miami stood out that year because Scandia Motorsport owner Andy Evans introduced one of the first World Sports Cars with a 4.5-liter displacement Buick V6-powered Kudzu. The Scandia entry was joined in the new open-cockpit category by team owner Brent O'Neill and his Buick-Argo. They would be the first of the cars that would become the main prototype category in 1994. Added purse bonuses encouraged entrants to get ahead of the curve and bring cars as they became available in anticipation of the following season's change in the configuration of the top prototypes.

Though not competitive overall with the big GTPs, the Buick-powered cars fit in well with the Lights. Entrants were pleased to be able to race them, to win a little extra purse money for those running flat-bottom cars, and to figure out how they worked with open cockpits and without full underbody aero tunnels as used by their GTP and Lights brethren. The Scandia Motorsport team of Evans would finish the season tenth in points in GTP—with a WSC car!

## THE EVERGREEN CONTRACT

By George Silbermann

Cigarettes may have been the most successful commercial product in the history of mankind. The cost to produce a pack of cigarettes was a tiny fraction of the retail price, even after accounting for crushing federal, state, and local taxes.

While a cowboy known as the Marlboro Man may have become a cultural icon representing the cigarette brand owned by Philip Morris & Co., chief rival R. J. Reynolds Tobacco was a more profitable company. In the 1980s, Reynolds Tobacco diversified by buying Nabisco Brands, and the new RJR Nabisco company then became the target of high-profile hostile takeovers. These efforts entered popular lore and remain case studies in business schools. They also inspired the 1989 book *Barbarians at the Gate*, which spawned a television movie adaptation.

In 1970, Junior Johnson introduced Reynolds Tobacco to NASCAR owner Bill France Sr. because he felt the company's size and the company's Winston brand, which sponsored NASCAR's premier Cup Series, warranted a much bigger opportunity than just sponsorship of his race team. IMSA became one of the collateral beneficiaries of that relationship when the Camel brand formally began its sponsorship of the GT series championship in 1972.

Reynolds Tobacco restricted itself from advertising in many areas during the latter decades of the twentieth century—by law in some cases. Just as often, the company was guided by internal policies, its legal department, and the fear that a hammer would come down hard if boundaries were overstepped at a time of widening enlightenment about the effects of smoking. Banned from television advertising, the company chose to focus its marketing efforts on sports. After creating a sports marketing division, Reynolds Tobacco became an event marketing pioneer, often promoting events that appeared on TV. Incredibly cash-heavy at the time, the company spent lavishly on motorsports of all types.

Like some other IMSA sponsors, Reynolds Tobacco officials were troubled by the 1989 sale of IMSA to Mike Cone and Jeff Parker and the new trajectory that the sanctioning body seemed to be taking. But the company still considered its relationship with IMSA an asset.

Its entitlement contract with IMSA was a multiyear "evergreen" arrangement, adding one additional year onto the long-term contract at the completion of each racing season. This clause had been put into place years before as a precaution, but in the 1990s it took on a different meaning altogether.

As the IMSA GTP era moved towards a close, Reynolds Tobacco was also staring at pending legislation that would fully restrict its promotional options, such as IMSA racing. Officials needed to end the evergreen contract with IMSA, but in the process did not want to not tear down the sport the Camel sponsorship had helped build. The officials in the marketing department hoped that a contract buyout, which would undoubtedly include a substantial financial settlement, would help keep the sport going after their departure.

Despite the best intentions, that is not how things eventually worked out. An agreement was reached with the IMSA owner, Reynolds Tobacco departed at the end of the 1993 season, and the sanctioning body saw none of the settlement money. When Charles Slater bought IMSA not long after the final deal had been struck, neither did he.

This is what the next generation Porsche 962 might have looked like had GTP continued in 1994. *IMSA Archive*

## OLDS VS. NISSAN

The Exxon Supreme GTS Series remained a seesaw battle between the Cunningham Nissan 300ZX Turbos driven by Millen and O'Connell against the Bob Riley–designed Oldsmobile Cutlasses of Gentilozzi and Brassfield. This time, Olds came out on top of the manufacturer championship, scoring six wins to two by the Nissan men and one by the reigning Ford Mustang Roush squad and driver Tommy Kendall. A year of steady finishes brought Kendall the driver's championship, his first major title following his huge accident at Watkins Glen in the Intrepid GTP car in 1991. He never finished worse than fifth in the nine-race GTS championship.

The GTO class for American V8s was dominated by the Olds Cutlass. Rob Morgan won the title after three sprint race wins compared with two by Joe Pezza. Les Lindley's Ford Mustang also captured two wins.

The Leitzinger Nissan team posted another clinic in GTU by winning six of the nine rounds and the Exxon-backed championship, this time led by second-generation driver Butch Leitzinger. Three wins went to the Mazda camp. Major victories were scored at the 24 Hours of Daytona and the 12 Hours of Sebring by the team of Dick Greer, Peter Uria, and Al Bacon. Bill Auberlen, chosen as the most improved driver while behind the wheel of his RX-7, won the enduro at Road America.

At Laguna Seca, the much-anticipated Allard GTP/Group C car ran for the first time anywhere. Looking completely different than anything else, it would have fit right in on a 2016 grid—but it was a spaceship in 1993! High downforce from both the underside and upper bodywork made the car unique.

Unfortunately, a 3.5-liter Cosworth V8 was simply not powerful enough to overcome the extra drag that the body design created along with the downforce. The car was premature in that regard. Plans to install a bigger turbo engine of some sort never came to fruition. Had it come about, the Allard would have been a very interesting and competitive package.

On the GT front, the continuation of the "international" became more solid in GT with IMSA recognizing a growing interest in the production-based "invitational GT" category at the four endurance races (Daytona, Sebring, Watkins Glen, and Road America). These production-based race cars were the leading edge of the future and attracted Porsche, Corvette, and most uniquely Jaguar. After a new Porsche Carrera 2 from Europe won the class in Daytona, a factory built and prepared Brumos Porsche Turbo made its debut at Sebring and stormed to first in class and seventh overall. Chasing the bigger, more powerful GTS cars from Nissan and Ford, this Porsche finished ahead of the Rocketsports Olds entries. At Watkins Glen, a Tommy Morrison–owned Mobil 1 Corvette took the win. Rounding out a diverse group of winners, Davy Jones and Jay Cochran drove their Jaguar XJ220 roadgoing supercar to tenth overall and the class win at Road America under sponsorship from Snap-on Tools.

It became clear the purpose-built tube frame cars in GTS and GTO were too strong to attempt total integration with these newer production-based cars. In GTU, however, the writing was on the wall for a future where convergence of these two types of cars would become a successful reality.

Wayne Taylor raced a privately entered Chevrolet Intrepid. It plagued the team with issues caused by its use of steel brakes instead of the original carbon discs. *IMSA Archive*

## SUPPORT SERIES STAND OUT

The 1993 season proved engaging for all four support series programs. Kenny Bräck, the year's outstanding newcomer and future Indy 500 winner, won the Zerex-sponsored Saab Series over Brandon Sperling and Alex Padilla, securing the $100,000 prize. The equally prepared, identical Saab-powered cars provided intense competition and a first glimpse of future stars. Future NASCAR standout Jerry Nadeau and Diego Guzman were other notable contenders.

The *Automobile Magazine* International Sedan Challenge was captured by veteran Irv Hoerr. Driving a new Oldsmobile Achieva as well as the older Calais model, he beat teammate Chuck Hemmingson, two-time winner Pepe Pombo driving a Nissan, and Acura Integra regular John Lewis. Averaging only sixteen cars per race and with only five races scheduled, this was a long-running IMSA series that would soon fall by the wayside as Firestone Firehawk and Bridgestone Supercar programs continued to grow and became more attractive to racers.

Year two of the Bridgestone Supercar Series was an exciting sophomore season. Factory-supported Porsche, Lotus, and BMW teams were mixing it up with numerous other entries: Corvette LT-1s, hot-rod Pontiac Firehawks, RX-7 Turbo IIs, and Saleen Mustangs. Plus, there was a Stillen aftermarket Nissan 300ZX Turbo. Hans Stuck, the Porsche ace from Germany, blew everyone away by winning the final seven races. Doc Bundy and David Murry scored one victory each in the Lotus Esprit X180R at the outset of the season. A race in conjunction with CART at Burke Lakefront Airport in Cleveland was an interesting plus for the series. The Supercars provided a welcome close-wheeled show to the open-wheel CART program that was usually headlined by Indy cars.

For those not familiar with the Burke Lakefront Airport, it was broad and flat with virtually no visual reference points. One of the more entertaining incidents of the race came on the Supercar pace lap. With the full field behind him, the pace car driver made a wrong turn, and everyone followed him off course, headed in the wrong direction on a similar-looking runway/taxiway. After some coaching from race control from its elevated position, where all this could be seen developing, the pace car and field were able to rejoin the actual racetrack and eventually the race got started.

The Firestone Firehawk Series continued to amaze. The first race at Sebring drew eighty-one entries for the twin three-hour races and fifty-seven for the mid-season Watkins Glen round. The season finale at Sebring drew seventy-nine entries for the combined classes that raced together for an impressive twelve hours. In the GS class, a season-long battle developed between the Porsche 944 S2 and the Pontiac Firebird Formula. The Pontiac army prevailed, winning all but two events on the nine-race calendar. Porsche took honors at the Sebring opener and closer with the 944s. Doug Goad and Larry Schumacher won the points championship over a notable field of competitors that included David Murry, Stu Hayner, John Heinricy, and Dave White.

The Honda Prelude VTEC and Honda Prelude Si proved to be the cars to beat in the Sports and Touring categories, respectively. Both the Honda models were ideal out-of-the-box showroom stock cars. They were fast, dependable, strong when it came to safety in in crashes (which happened a lot), and very enjoyable to drive.

Peter Schwartzott claimed the driver title in Sports with three wins in his Honda VTEC, compared to Joe Danaher's five victories in Mazda RX-7 Turbo II and Olds Achieva entries. Touring class champion John Green outlasted Lance Stewart, Norris Rancourt, Mitch Payton, and Earwood to win the title in a Prelude Si.

The task of racing a pure street legal car as fast as it can go for hours on end had the tendency to sort out which makes and models could do it and

The Firestone Firehawk Endurance Championship enjoyed huge fields and rambunctious competition in every category. *Peter Gloede*

which could not. Manufacturers learned very quickly what designs and parts would last. Proving the product on the track was an easy and inexpensive way to test designs and learn what to improve. Many car manufacturers' engineers caught the racing bug, got racing licenses, and experienced for themselves the real quality, or lack thereof, of their product.

Though there was not the diversity up front, at times the racing between teams in the leading cars proved to be as exciting to watch as any form of racing. And racing what people could buy in showrooms made sense. As much as competitors loved to brag, after the fact, about how they "bent" the rules (or in some instances simply cheated) in showroom stock racing, the reality was different. For eight seasons, Sun Electric and its diagnostic machines had been a fixture in the Firehawk paddock for prerace and postrace technical analysis. Many competitors were grateful for the way the Sun technicians pointed out to them how to bring their cars up to their fullest potential.

Under IMSA Vice President Silbermann's direction, the technical requirements calling for completely stock specifications were strongly enforced. This resulted in many cars going home on a regular

Competing in the Barber Saab Pro Series, Derek Hill tested his skills in the Mondial chassis powered by a Saab four-cylinder turbo. *Rick Dole*

basis with their engines and transmissions loaded into cardboard boxes in parts. A select few were found to be so far off their cars' specification that they were thrown out of the series completely.

Compliance and postrace tech may have been draconian at times, but it set a tone of total compliance at the risk of results getting thrown out. There were statistics kept internally at IMSA on who had been thrown out most often. While mostly for grins, it did give officials a good idea of who needed more scrutiny. Competitors were tossed for almost anything one can think of: lightened pistons; valve and port machining; removable roll cages that were not removable; wrong brakes; interior paneling removed; ECUs that had been re-chipped; and on and on . . . It showed over time that the most successful competitors were the ones who executed the race the best, with a properly prepared car. Those bending or even warping the rules demonstrated that it made little difference at this level.

There was no more power to be had, no gearing to change, no weight savings allowed. Buy the make and model of your choice from the eligibility list, bolt in a roll cage, take out the spare tire and jack, put in a racing seat and belts, and add a small fire extinguisher. Slap some numbers and a series decal kit on it, maybe paint it . . . Then go race it.

Behind the scenes at IMSA, Greenwood brought a calming atmosphere both internally and in the paddock. Staff and competitors found him easy to talk to. He recognized he still had one of the best operational groups anywhere in motorsports and provided valuable common-sense input when needed or asked, but he let his people do their jobs without interference.

Greenwood managed owner Cone and had dedicated support from board members Bishop and Cooper. Over the course of the season, some staffers noticed Cone's waning interest. He really did not know much about racing or IMSA specifically, but he continued to involve himself in decision-making in a way that often did more damage

Rain at Sebring could make a challenging course treacherous. *Brian Cleary*

The Allard J2X-C made its lone appearance in the Laguna Seca round. A Cosworth engine could not overcome a reported 8,000 pounds of downforce. *Costas Los Collection*

than good. Once again, the rumors started that he was interested in selling IMSA. He continuously denied this to the board, the media, and anyone of means who suggested an interest in purchasing the company.

The Camel GT ended with the season finale in Phoenix. Jones and Fangio raced door-to-door into the sunset for a thrilling end to the Camel GT's fantastic story. The AAR Toyota teammates finished one-two in seven of the eleven races, and each had only one DNF all year. In addition to Fangio's $500,000 in purse and point fund money, Jones took home $240,000 in winnings for his runner-up finish.

Moretti finished third in the points and was recognized for his record of 150 race starts in the overall category in the Camel GT. He was

The new Bridgestone Supercar Championship attracted top level talent. Hans Stuck drove the Porsche 930 Turbo for Brumos Racing. *Lee Self*

presented with an original portrait showing all the different MOMO-liveried cars he had raced in the series.

In the preceding decades, the Camel GT showcased the world's fastest and most exotic road racing sports cars, attracted some of the

finest road racing drivers from around the world, and had honored champions like Peter Gregg, Brian Redman, John Fitzpatrick, John Paul Jr., Al Holbert, Chip Robinson, Geoff Brabham, and Juan Manuel Fangio II. Most importantly, the racing thrilled hundreds of thousands of fans at the track and on worldwide television. At the close of the season, it was all in the record books. For 1994, the Exxon World Sports Car Series would be the new category, along with the Exxon Supreme GT Series.

## LAST MEN STANDING

By George Silbermann

In 1993, IMSA was well into its transition from GTP to the new World Sports Car formula. A handful of IMSA GTP entries competed in the final year of the category. Almost all were privateers. There was only one factory-backed team remaining: Dan Gurney's All American Racers and its two-car Toyota effort that featured two primary drivers of impressive racing lineage. Juan Manuel Fangio II was named after his uncle, a five-time time Formula One World Champion. P. J. Jones was the son of Indy 500 legend and off-road icon Parnelli Jones.

The cars may have been the most advanced endurance racing machines ever created. Stories circulated that the potent Toyotas no longer used their turbochargers to boost engine output. Instead, it was somehow the other way around. The engine powered the turbos that then served as the primaries in some exotic new propulsion method, one that resulted in incredible power.

Racing myths notwithstanding, the two AAR Toyotas were spectacular everywhere they raced, including at a circuit that few in the world of sports cars might have anticipated. The track was in Georgia, but it was not Road Atlanta.

Instead, the IMSA Camel GT event took place at Atlanta Motor Speedway, the high-banked oval that was built for NASCAR races and renowned for its wickedly fast stock car racing speeds as well as Indy cars. Shortly after purchasing the track, owner Bruton Smith had installed a "roval" configuration with an infield road course, which enabled him to add one of the Camel GT races to his schedule. The infield was just as wicked, in its own way, as the steeply banked oval that made up a good portion of the roval layout.

IMSA support series events that were run earlier, like the Firestone Firehawk Endurance Championship, were almost scary to watch, but the AAR Toyotas put on a show for the ages in the main race. Any constraints that had been placed on Fangio and Jones about racing each other very hard in Toyota's final season of GTP racing seemed to have been lifted (if they had ever really been there in the first place . . .). The two drivers took their GTP cars to the limit and dueled with each other in a truly amazing spectacle. Fangio came out on top that day. Months later, Jones would come out on top after a similarly dazzling battle with Fangio at yet another roval, this time at Phoenix International Raceway.

Gurney and All American Racers won every race that season, except the Road America round won by the Joest Racing team, which marked the final victory for a Porsche 962 and summed up the longevity, diversity, and excitement of the GTP category. The AAR team swept the championship with Fangio II crowned as the final Camel GTP title winner. With one final roar, it was the end of an era and the dawning of another.

## HEADED FOR THE CARIBBEAN

By Mark Raffauf

Starting in the late 1970s, a large contingent of drivers and teams from the Caribbean basin began competing in IMSA's Florida races, sometimes continuing for a full Camel GT season. By the late 1980s, the amount of IMSA GT hardware used by these teams and drivers to race in their home countries was sufficient for organizers in the Caribbean region to start their own local GT series.

Championships in Costa Rica and Puerto Rico along with events in other countries in the region

The racers who competed around the Caribbean basin in the Marlboro GT Series often raced each other in IMSA.
*Mark Raffauf*

were based on the practical and cost-effective tube frame IMSA GT designs. Starting in late 1992 with a visit to Costa Rica at the invitation of Max Mosley—who would become the FIA president the following year—IMSA worked with other officials and representatives to help create an FIA-sanctioned series in the Caribbean region called the Marlboro GT of the Americas.

This new international series was another significant step forward for Latin American racers in IMSA. In its early days, officials at IMSA were warned by another American road racing sanctioning body that Latin American racers were unreliable, did not pay their bills, and caused agitation in the paddock. IMSA found the exact opposite to be true. The Latin American participants loved to race and were reliable,

The 300ZX Nissan Turbo of Clayton Cunningham Racing lined up for practice with an ex-IMSA Pontiac Fiero next door. *Mark Raffauf*

polite, friendly, and fast. These drivers and their teams were welcome additions to IMSA.

The initial foray into IMSA was led by Dominican Luis Rafael Méndez, who was the 1980 IMSA GTO champion, and Puerto Rican Diego Febles. Many other drivers and teams ventured into the IMSA fold over the years. Febles was one of the few who could buy used race cars from Peter Gregg, due to their friendship, and he regularly purchased new Porsche RSRs. The Brumos team allowed Febles to run its classic red and blue stripe livery, but he used No. 58 instead of the iconic No. 59.

Febles would eventually sell the Porsches to fellow Caribbean competitors, increasing the IMSA car population in the region. In 1975, a commemorative 24 Hours of Daytona poster printed by Porsche was

Peruvian Eduardo Dibos and his Mazda MX6 participated in IMSA events in South America and around the Caribbean.
*Mark Raffauf*

headlined "Triumph of Reliability" and featured four RSRs crossing the finish line, led by the No. 59 Brumos car. At one time or another, he owned three of those Porsches.

During the 1970s, Febles mortgaged his house and his auto repair business in Puerto Rico and used some of his son's college education fund to compete in the entire Camel GT schedule. His wife Maria and son Tony were initially unaware of how the racing was being funded and were not pleased when they found out. Diego, on the other hand, thought it was a great idea! Over the course of the season, his team spent slightly over $29,000 and won $32,000 in prize money, which kept everybody in the family happy. Diego's famous line at the racetrack was, "Estamos en el billete!," which translates to "We are in the money."

Drivers from Puerto Rico, the Dominican Republic, Venezuela, Colombia, Peru, Panama, and Mexico were regulars on IMSA starting grids. In 1980, Méndez won the GTO Championship outright in a strong season-long campaign in his Porsche Carrera crewed by his wife and two mechanics, beating the likes of Bob Tullius and Group 44's Triumph TR8s. Mauricio de Narváez won the 12 Hours of Sebring

The GTS class Roush Mustangs, built in Venezuela, were standouts on the grid. *Mark Raffauf*

in 1984 along with co-drivers Stefan Johansson and Hans Heyer in a Porsche 935 on loan from Reinhold Joest's collection in Germany. Eduardo Dibos ran successfully in GT cars and eventually in a WSC Prototype in the 1990s. There were many more . . .

The move from various series in the Caribbean basin to a fully sanctioned international FIA championship was pushed by Mosley, who invited IMSA and the Automobile Club of the US (ACCUS) to participate in an inaugural meeting in San Jose, Costa Rica, in December 1992. The following year, a series of meetings was held in San Jose and Miami, some of which were attended by Mark Raffauf of IMSA and ACCUS President Berdie Martin, in addition to FIA representatives and event promoters from each country that wanted to participate in a recognized championship. The result was a series called the *Marlboro GT of the Americas* that was based on IMSA's GTO/GTS and GTU regulations. There was already an ample supply of current and slightly older cars running regularly in each country's national races.

Costa Rican promoter Gustavo Pacheco brought Marlboro sponsorship to the concept. With support

Mark Honsowetz and the Clayton Cunningham Racing crew joined the competition in the Caribbean. *Mark Raffauf*

The wide-open spaces of the Maracaibo, Venezuela, circuit offered fans and participants ample views of the entire track.
*Mark Raffauf*

from IMSA's George Silbermann and Raffauf, he was able to bring representatives from other countries to the table and explain the benefits of a unified series that would operate under one set of rules as opposed to individual events being run to different regulations and influenced by local politics. With Philip Morris's top brand ready to step up to a series sponsorship, Pacheco explained that if everyone could agree to get along and work together, something good could happen.

From 1993 to 1996, this annual calendar of Marlboro-backed GT events was supported almost exclusively by tube frame GTO/GTS/GTU cars that were built to a rule book that was originally established by IMSA. Good promotion and huge crowds were the norm, confirming the love of racing by Latin fans. IMSA regulars from the Caribbean basin were strong supporters, including Febles, Méndez, Kikos Fonseca, Wally Castro, Mandy Gonzalez, Biaggio Parisi, Manolo Villa, Adriano Abreu, Bonky Fernandez, and many others. These drivers' names were also spread through IMSA race results for decades.

Some IMSA regulars made the trip south, usually going down in the late fall prior to the preparations needed for the 24 Hours of Daytona. In weather perfect for racing, they experienced the excitement of tropical destinations and big crowds of enthusiastic spectators. This group included Irv Hoerr, Tommy Riggins, Johnny O'Connell, and John Morton, the latter two co-driving one of Clayton Cunningham's 300ZX Turbos. The IMSA competitors' cars were usually sold to the series regulars and subsequently supported from the US as needed. This steady flow of complete cars and parts to series participants helped support a lot of the IMSA teams and their US-based racing businesses.

Venezuela's Parisi went a step further and brought down a group of experienced mechanics and fabricators from south Florida who were familiar with IMSA's cars. Along with their Venezuelan counterparts, they built four Roush Mustangs in the basement of the Parisi family pasta factory in Maracaibo, Venezuela.

Maravilloso. Ese fue el calificativo empleado por Mark Raffauf, vice presidente ejecutivo de la serie norteamericana IMSA al apreciar el ambiente que mostraba el autódromo Los Parisi de Maracaibo en la última válida del primer GT Marlboro de las Américas. Fue la culminación de ocho meses de competencias entre los mejores pilotos de Puerto Rico, Panamá, República Dominicana, Costa Rica y Venezuela, los cuales se enfrentaron en nueve oportunidades en siete autódromos de cinco naciones caribeñas.

Bajo la tutela deportiva de Nacam-Fisa y el respaldo económico de Marlboro, el éxito del Nacam GT se evidenció mejor que nunca en la prueba de cierre realizada en autódromo Los Parisi de Maracaibo, en donde se hicieron presentes 40 pilotos representantes de 8 naciones y 22 máquinas con una potencia acumulada de 10.000 caballos de fuerza. En la prolongada recta del caluroso autódromo zuliano se registraron marcas cercanas a los 300 kph, cifras escalofriantes para nuestro automovilismo.

Desde los primeros ensayos libres se evidenció la superioridad del Nissan ZX300 biturbo. El vehículo japonés se presentó con una infraestructura notable, en la que destacaban 6 mecánicos norteamericanos y la presencia del piloto oficial Nissan-USA, Johnny O'Conell además del costarricense Roberto Tinoco.

El viernes, a final de la tarde, el pelirrojo corredor americano aprovechó un descenso en la temperatura para marcar el mejor registro, y fue tal la seguridad exhibida por el equipo Nissan que ni se molestaron en salir a clasificar el sábado, concentrándose en los detalles para la carrera.

El dominicano Luis Rafael Méndez, líder del campeonato, había visto anular su tiempo del viernes al no presentarse en el pesaje, mientras el sábado un incendio casi consume el Oldsmobile Cutlass destacándose la rápida intervención del equipo de seguridad comandado por Heduardo Rodríguez.

Menos suerte tuvo el tico Kikos Fonseca quien pulverizó el motor del Chevrolet Corvette en los entrenamientos libres del sábado, viéndose obligado a desistir de la carrera.

Veinte máquinas tomaron parte en las 2 Horas de Venezuela

# METEORO DE AMÉRICA

Octavio Estrada

*EL VENEZOLANO BIAGGIO "METEORO" PARISI DOMINÓ A PLACER LA PARTE FINAL DEL PRIMER GT MARLBORO DE LAS AMÉRICAS, UN TORNEO ESPECTACULAR CON UN INCREÍBLE DESENLACE*

NEWSPORTS

88

...ETEORO?

## A 40° CENTÍGRADOS

Veinte máquinas se formaron en la parrilla de salida y antes de completar la primera vuelta de calentamiento, el "reloj" 21 de Antonio Bettencourt entraba a los pits con problemas en el turbo. Lo que jamás ocurrió durante el año se presentó en una competencia que por sus características, le habría asegurado un lugar en el podio. Pero éste fue apenas el primero de la larga lista de abandonos. En la primera vuelta de la carrera el Chevrolet Beretta de la pareja argentino-española (ambos con licencia americana) Daniel Urrutia-Luis Seriex se quedaban con inconvenientes en el motor, repitiendo así la efímera presentación de Turagua. El Oldsmobile del dominicano Adriano Abreu, que compartía la primera fila con el Nissan, también se detuvo con un caucho delantero pinchado.

Con un ritmo demoledor el Nissan de Johnny O'Conell acumulaba una considerable ventaja sobre Biaggio Parisi, el cual estaba enfrascado en una lucha con el Camaro Marlboro de Mandy González, ganador en Maracaibo de la edición internacional del 92. Por su parte el americano Irv Hoerr, compañero de Luis Rafael Méndez, le puso emoción al asunto y en la primera media hora logró escalar hasta la tercera posición, esfuerzo que concluyó poco antes de cumplirse la mitad de la prueba con el motor pulverizado, y con él, las esperanzas del dominicano Méndez por conquistar la corona. Este retiro liberaba al equipo Nissan y a su nuevo piloto Roberto Tinoco de la presión por mantenerse en la primera posición, concentrándose en la obtención del título. Biaggio Parisi aprovechó el reabastecimiento del Nissan para irse al frente, postergando su parada hasta pasada la primera hora de carrera. Meteoro sacó una vuelta de ventaja al costarricense frente a la tribuna principal, lo que generó una explosión de júbilo por parte de las casi 7000 personas que llenaron las gradas del autódromo.

Apenas un ligero retraso en el cambio del neumático trasero derecho y el Mustang Marlboro de Parisi volvió a la pista todavía en el primer lugar, sin embargo lo impredecible ocurrió pocas vueltas después, al reventarse precisamente el caucho posterior derecho, que obligó al zuliano a recorrer medio circuito a un ritmo muy lento antes de parar en pits. Tinoco recuperó la punta de la carrera, aunque su ritmo conservador propició la recuperación de Biaggio. Un trompo sin consecuencias de Tinoco facilitó la tarea de Parisi quien pasó nuevamente al frente en menos de 10 vueltas.

Todo parecía definido a falta de 40 minutos para el final de la carrera. Tinoco, con el campeonato asegurado, debía entregar el volante a su compañero para la parte final, pero a su entrada a

Biaggio Parisi venció con cuatro vueltas de ventaja

... González de la prueba. El norteamericano Ken Bopp pasó de revoluciones el Camaro de Maurizio Scala y ello les costó todo el fin de semana trabajando en el ocho cilindros, terminando justo a tiempo para la carrera.

El asfixiante calor del asfalto zuliano preocupaba a todos los participantes invitados. El debutante equipo colombiano programaba hasta tres cambios de piloto, mientras el rapidísimo Johnny O'Conell no salía de su asombro al enterarse de que Biaggio Parisi correría solo al igual que Antonio Bettencourt.

Todo estaba listo para el gran evento, el cual presentaba un ingrediente adicional para todo el ambiente venezolano: por primera vez veríamos reabastecimientos en los pits, razón por la cual se habilitó el pasillo que usualmente se emplea en las competencias de piques, un detalle -si se quiere insignificante- que cambiaría la historia del torneo.

Los dos carros colombianos llegaron segundos en GTS y GTU

NEWSPORTS

89

Regional sports publications and television carried regular coverage of every race in the Marlboro GT of the Americas. *IMSA Archive*

Outfitted with Roush-built V8 Fords, they were equal to anything running in IMSA. The Parisi pasta factory made pasta for almost all of Venezuela and Colombia, but little was known about the full-blown race shop and Roush Mustangs assembled in the basement!

Throughout this period, the Marlboro Series participants continued to enter IMSA events in Florida and elsewhere. They were among the top performers in the Exxon GT Supreme Series in the GTS, GTO, and GTU categories.

The connection to this series also produced cars competing in the Camel GT with classic red and white chevrons of Marlboro for the first time in series history. This was unusual since R. J. Reynolds did not allow a competing tobacco company to participate as a sponsor. The unidentified red chevrons merely suggested Marlboro for the initiated but did not qualify as an actual sponsor. For the previous twenty-three years under Reynolds Tobacco's Camel banner (and one year with Winston), the famed chevron of Phillip Morris had never been seen at an IMSA event.

The first Marlboro GT of the Americas Series in 1993 consisted of nine events: two each in Puerto Rico, Costa Rica, the Dominican Republic, and Venezuela, plus one in Panama. The races lasted one, two, or three hours with full pit stops. Luis Méndez was crowned champion, having driven his US-built Oldsmobile Cutlass, which was virtually identical to the IMSA GTO title-winning car of Hoerr. Méndez won three races, including one where he was co-driving with car-builder Hoerr at the La Cumbre circuit in Bonao, Dominican Republic. IMSA Nissan GTS driver Johnny O'Connell won two races co-driving the first Clayton Cunningham–built customer car, which was owned by Panamanian Roberto Tinoco. Parisi won two in his Venezuelan-built Roush Ford Mustang, and Abreu won two in another US-built Cutlass.

A seven-race calendar was contested in 1994 in the Dominican Republic, Puerto Rico, Venezuela, and Costa Rica. Morton teamed with Tinoco in the potent 300ZX Turbo to win round three in Maracaibo, Venezuela. Parisi won another round in one of his Venezuelan Mustangs. Castro and Rolando Falgueras were also driving a Venezuelan-built Mustang; they won the season opener and captured the championship with steady finishes all season.

The 1995 schedule had eight events, including one at a new venue in Colombia. Castro and Falgueras once again won the Marlboro GT Championship of the Americas in their Mustang by winning three races. Co-drivers Gonzales and Villa won one event, as did Méndez and the Abreu team. Tinoco scored two victories, once with O'Connell and once with Morton co-driving. Four different IMSA-spec cars won races: the Olds Cutlass, Ford Mustang, Chevrolet Camaro, and Nissan 300ZX Turbo.

The competition was always close, the events well promoted and managed, but ultimately the increasing worldwide pressure on tobacco companies' sponsorship and promotion activities forced Marlboro to leave at the end of 1995. The series continued for one more season and is known to many of the participants as "the golden age of Creole motorsports." Having been inspired and nurtured by IMSA, the series was professionally executed by the participants and the FIA-sanctioned national sporting authorities of each country.

As the 1990s wore on, many involved in motorsports in other parts of the world continued to turn to IMSA for guidance and direction, which was always forthcoming whenever possible. In 2013, IMSA founder Bishop was inducted posthumously into the Caribbean Motorsports Hall of Fame located in the Museum of Transportation in Guaynabo, Puerto Rico. Two years later, Raffauf became the second American from the Continental US to be inducted into the Caribbean Motorsports Hall of Fame.

EXXON

MOTOROLA
GTE
03
Oil Changer
WHEEL WORKS
EXXON

GTE
Mobilnet
2
MOTOROLA
EXXON

CHAPTER FIVE

# 1994: WORLD SPORTS CARS TAKE OVER

Long before the final races of the Camel GTP and Camel Lights series, it became clear that the formula was unsustainable. A new approach to prototypes was needed for IMSA's premier category.

To create this new approach, retired sanctioning body founder John Bishop began meeting with IMSA Vice Presidents Silbermann and Raffauf in 1992. The goal was to give participating teams an opportunity to win the major races and the championship without having to rely on major factory backing. The target date for the launch of the new prototypes was the 1994 season-opening Rolex 24 at Daytona.

As it turned out, the 1994 season began with the arrival of a new owner as well. Unbeknownst to the staff, Mike Cone sold the sanctioning body early in the year and Charles Slater was introduced as the new owner shortly after the Rolex 24.

There was no announcement on the actual date of sale, nor was there much known about the new owner. Thirty-five-year-old Slater had competed in several Daytona and Sebring events without much distinction, other than being black-flagged for being too slow at his first 12 Hours of Sebring. He and two partners had recently sold their high-tech medical hardware company, Symbiosis Corp., which made Slater a multimillionaire. While vintage racing, he met Hal Kelley, who persuaded him to consider buying IMSA. Kelley made a subsequent introduction to Cone, which led to the purchase. In retrospect, it was one neophyte to the business of racing selling the sanctioning body to another newcomer, one who would initially rely on Kelley for guidance.

On the car side, larger economic questions in the auto industry combined with the unsustainable financial demands for manufacturers and competing teams in the GTP and Lights categories meant

Brix Racing doubled down on its Spice-Olds entries. Jeremy Dale drove the No. 2 car to four victories, but he fell three points shy of the inaugural WSC Championship. *Randy McKee*

that a fresh start was needed. Given the ongoing demise of the world championship of the FIA's Group C, sustaining the top classes of sports car racing was an international challenge. In the US, a major change was needed to confirm a distinct new direction amid the growing uncertainty within the motorsports industry about Cone's commitment to IMSA.

On the positive side, the Exxon Supreme GT Series had gained traction under the sponsorship of Exxon and its high-performance gasoline brand. Officials at Exxon found their investment to be working well enough to consider taking on the title sponsorship of a new prototype class in addition to the GT Series. This would coincide with the introduction of Exxon's high-octane,

At the dawn of the World Sports Car era, Spices powered by a Chevy V8 and an Olds V8 started on the front row at Daytona. *Brian Cleary*

Speed and reliability were the hallmarks of the powerful Nissan 300 ZX Turbo of Clayton Cunningham Racing. *NASCAR Archive and Research Center*

unleaded racing gasolines that would be used by all competitors.

With additional title sponsorship in place, the new formula became the Exxon World Sports Car Championship (WSC). Instead of two classes, there was a single category for open-cockpit prototypes—based on similar chassis to the Lights class—that called for production-based engines. It proved to be an inviting economic platform for both privateers and manufacturers, producing full grids very soon after the launch at Daytona.

The cars were strong, fast, and far more cost effective to campaign. Fans liked seeing and easily identifying the drivers in the open cockpits—useful in a style of racing where drivers were regularly changed on pit stops. The WSC class proved sustainable and would have a long-running influence in both IMSA and sports prototype endurance racing around the world into the early 2000s.

When it came to designing a new type of car, meetings were held with those interested in pursuing a new way to go IMSA racing. The conversation

The writing was on the wall and on top of the Daytona scoring tower. Nissan's GTS-class CCR entry led the Porsche Turbos of Brumos and Labre. *Brian Cleary*

At the outset of the 1994 season, Charlie Slater became the third IMSA owner in five years. *Brian Doc Mitchell*

started with the existing Camel Lights cars. These prototypes used smaller engines and carried less weight compared to the larger, faster, and more expensive GTP machines, making them an ideal basis for a less expensive car.

A Camel Lights car's "ground effect" tunnels on the underside could be replaced with a flat-bottom chassis. By eliminating the pursuit of improving "ground effect" aerodynamics, wind tunnel testing of underbodies and its related expenses could be cut. ("Ground effect," of course, was a misnomer. It was the routing of air through tunnels on the underside of the car that created downward pressure and helped the car hug the track.)

With an eye on emphasizing driver skill and budgets, the rule book called for narrower tires.

By requiring production-based engines and eliminating turbocharging, development costs could be reduced in another area where entrants tended to spend a lot of money. The rules limited engines with two-valve cylinder heads to 5.0 liters, engines with multi-valve heads to 4.0 liters, and Mazdas to three rotors.

To encourage early adoption by team owners, purse bonuses were announced for WSC cars that would participate during the final GTP/Lights season of 1993. Existing Lights chassis, such as the Argo and Kudzu, were modified to become the first WSC entries. The roofs were cut off and the roll hoop structures around the open cockpits were reinforced with front and rear bracing. The tunneled underbodies were eliminated to meet the flat-bottom chassis rule. Other modified Lights class entries, such as Spice and Tiga, were converted by the time the 1994 season arrived.

The biggest new development was the interest of Ferrari, which confirmed the category's appeal as an opportunity to build and sell customer prototypes at a reasonable price.

Gianpiero Moretti of MOMO fame initially led the effort in Italy to convince Ferrari the time was right for a new "customer only" racing car.

Canadian Jeremy Dale piloting the Spice-Olds of Brix Racing, where Dave "Beaky" Sims commanded the crew.
*Brian Cleary*

The GTS-class Nissan outran all the new WSC entries in the Rolex 24. A new prototype class not winning its first race would become a Daytona tradition. *NASCAR Archive and Research Center*

Numerous visits by Moretti and Raffauf to the Ferrari factory in 1992 and 1993 cemented the decision by president Luca Montezemolo and vice president Piero Ferrari to proceed on the project, and the 333SP was born. Ferrari's commitment came with a reasonable political price: IMSA agreed to not change the regulations for the first year and to not allow turbos.

Until Ferrari became part of the equation, the acceptance of the WSC class in Europe was far from universal. The Le Mans organizers at the Automobile Club de l'Ouest (ACO) instead were focused on promoting relatively expensive GT1 cars as their top class for the future.

The first renderings of the new Ferrari prototype were released in 1993 and appeared on the cover of *AutoSprint* in Italy the same week as a press conference held in Paris by the ACO to promote the 24 Hours of Le Mans. Media members asked, given Ferrari's new sports car design, why this new prototype was not part of the ACO's future. By time the WSC cars were launched, the ACO had embraced the class by approving it for competition in its twenty-four hour. This gave the race a lower cost alternative for teams pursuing an overall win.

The Ferrari was conceived with power from the multi-valve Ferrari F50 road car's V12 engine, which in turn was derived from the 3.5-liter engine used in Formula One. Downsized to meet IMSA's maximum displacement for multi-valve engines of 4.0 liters, the designation of 333 came from traditional means at Ferrari—the volume of each cylinder's displacement (333 cubic centimeters). Paddock rumors suggested this was a pure race engine, but it was an available production powerplant in the F50.

Utilizing five valves per cylinder and a cast-iron block, the V12 turned 12,000 rpm, mesmerizing fans and participants with its glorious high-pitched

The Brumos Porsche 964 Turbo GT America was among the GTS entries trying to score a victory at Sebring.
*Brian Cleary*

Craig T. Nelson, who played "Coach" in the eponymous hit TV series, joined the Exxon World Sports Car Championship in a Spice with Lexus V8 power. *Brian Cleary*

roar. The car was magic and its winning introduction at Road Atlanta in April 1994 was a significant shot in the arm for continued growth in IMSA's new top category.

Starting with a sale to Moretti, the initial twelve Ferraris were immediately sold to IMSA or European racing customers. Each had to be purchased with a spares package that included an engine, gearbox, complete set of bodywork, and four separate suspension/brake corners. This helped keep collectors at bay, and for less than $1 million, a privateer was ready to race. Ferrari later confided that the 333SP was one of the most profitable cars in Ferrari's history.

The 333SP was entered in 144 races totaling 491 starts. They won forty-nine races and posted ninety-four podium finishes. The car's eligibility remained in place for ten years, achieving success well into the 2000s with the Grand-Am Series—including one chassis with a Judd V10 installed as a replacement to the aging V12 (hence the nickname of "the Fudd"). Moretti's most successful season came in 1998, when he won the Rolex 24 at Daytona, the 12 Hours of Sebring, the six-hour race at Watkins Glen, and recorded a third-place finish in the Prototype class and fourteenth overall at Le Mans on board his Ferrari.

With an eye toward beginning with shorter events, Ferrari did not introduce its new 333SP prototype until the third race of the 1994 campaign, a sprint for WSC prototypes only at Road Atlanta.

Spice and Kudzu joined Ferrari and they became the three principal constructors in WSC's first season. Constructors—like Lola—as well as several

The open cockpit design of WSC gave drivers and fans a new way of seeing the action. *Lee Self*

one-offs—such as Roger Mandeville's Hawk—also joined the competition. The original IMSA WSC-type car was a success and continued as a premier category for a decade, although a second-generation version under the Le Mans rule book arrived in 1998 with turbos, bigger engines, and more aerodynamics—the things IMSA purposely avoided at the outset to contain costs and make the class accessible to privateers.

The first purpose-built cars of the new category were from British constructor Spice Engineering. The company came to the US after establishing itself in FIA Group C and Group C2. Along with team owners Evans and Dyson in 1994, Harry Brix took up the Spice cause from the very beginning and stuck with it. His Oldsmobile-Spices were always contenders with Jeremy Dale as the lead driver until his unfortunate accident at Road Atlanta in 1995.

Downing's Mazda-Kudzu cars from the Camel Lights class were also a natural selection for adaptation to WSC, though slightly underpowered with a three-rotor engine (the only option because Mazda's four-rotor was judged to be too powerful). The Kudzu chassis were later fit with Buick V6 and eventually GM V8s for WSC competition.

James Weaver at the wheel of the Dyson Racing Spice, which featured a stock-based Ferrari V8. *Randy McKee*

## SUMMONED

By George Silbermann

The world took a different turn for everyone working at IMSA and in sports car racing shortly after the Rolex 24 at Daytona opened the 1994 season.

The day after the race, the staff was working at IMSA's Tampa headquarters to pursue the usual post-ace tasks, but unbeknownst to nearly everyone, owner Mike Cone had sold the business.

By late 1993, it was an open secret that Cone was looking to sell the sanctioning body. There had been the usual rumblings about several interested parties. During that race weekend, for example, IMSA executives Dan Greenwood and Mark Raffauf had met with a representative from a British group at Daytona to discuss this very topic.

IMSA's senior management learned about a completed sale for the first time on that fateful day after the Rolex as they were summoned, one by one, to a downtown Tampa hotel to meet the new owner, Charles Slater, and to learn their fates. It was like a scene from a bad movie. The first to be called was Greenwood, the IMSA president. An executive during the Olympic Games in Los Angeles and later the director of Riverside Raceway in California, he was an experienced motorsports man. His tenure at IMSA ended that afternoon.

New owner Slater was largely unknown in the IMSA garage or anywhere else in the motorsports industry. He chose Hal Kelley, who was a known quantity in IMSA circles, to replace Greenwood as the new IMSA president.

Kelley and his partner Scott Riley had organized the GTE World Challenge on a temporary circuit at the Tampa Fairgrounds in 1988, hoping for it to be an IMSA Camel GT championship event. There was already a glut of races on the calendar in Florida. Other event promoters, competitors, and officials from series sponsor R. J. Reynolds all cried foul at the idea of yet another one. The World Challenge was added as an invitational race between IMSA GTP cars and the European-based Group C cars, one that did not count as part of the Camel GT championship.

Cone and his associate Jeff Parker had been the two main financial backers of the World Challenge. It was largely believed that Kelley and Riley convinced

## A UNIQUE TRADITION UPHELD

The year 1994 was the first full season for WSC, and it started by upholding a unique tradition in the Rolex 24 at Daytona. Thanks to their reliability, the previous generation of cars had always beat the newcomers. In 1977, a Porsche Carrera RSR won the twenty-four-hour race over the company's vaunted new turbocharged 935s. It was a Porsche 935 that beat a strong field of GTP cars when that class made its debut at Daytona. A little more than a decade later, it would be no different as the powerful GTS class Nissan 300ZX Turbo beat all the WSC entries at the Rolex after they faltered with mechanical woes. Scott Pruett, Steve Millen, Paul Gentilozzi, and Butch Leitzinger drove the Clayton Cunningham–entered Nissan.

Brix's Oldsmobile-Spice finished ninth and claimed the first-in-class WSC points at Daytona. Brix drivers Dale, Melgrati, Cobb, and Bob Schader were closely followed by the Mazda-Kudzu entered by constructor Downing and co-driven by Wayne Taylor, Hugh Fuller, and Charles Morgan. With second-place class points, it was the beginning of Taylor's successful pursuit of the first WSC points championship.

The debut of the new Porsche 911 Turbo—entered by Larbre Competition, Brumos Porsche, and Champion Porsche—was a notable event. The European-based Larbre Competition team claimed second overall behind the winning Nissan. After a decade of class victories, team owner Jack Roush did not enter one of his Ford Mustangs, surprisingly,

the two Tampa businessmen to purchase IMSA from founder John Bishop. Once the sale of IMSA was completed in 1989, the World Challenge was converted to a points-paying Camel GT race, bringing the total number of Camel GT rounds in Florida to five. Kelley later resigned his post at the World Challenge, plus his role as a racing consultant, and went to work in a different industry. He had seemingly moved on from motorsports. Then he met Slater at vintage racing events, convinced him to buy IMSA from Cone, and suddenly was back on the scene as the new leader of IMSA.

Mark Raffauf was called to the hotel after Greenwood, followed by fellow vice president George Silbermann. Amos Johnson, the technical director, was next. The one-sided conversations at the hotel clearly indicated that Slater planned to clean house and install his own people, but a very weird day got even weirder. Contrary to the plan, executives Raffauf and Silbermann would end up continuing in their roles at IMSA. Kelley would go on to become the chief executive, albeit with the shortest term of any IMSA president once Slater later fired him.

Raffauf and Silbermann stayed on because of the influence of Slater's business affairs manager and lawyer, Dan White. Slater had discussed with others in the industry what would be the best way to move forward. Hal Kelley was the motivator behind Charlie's initial enthusiasm for becoming the sanctioning body owner and was a known entity for many. Dan White's insight regarding the self-serving role played by Kelley along with a healthy respect for those already doing all the work led to both Raffauf and Silbermann being asked to stay, with the understanding that they would work under Kelley's direction. Kelley lasted less than a year before being dismissed, and Silbermann took over the president's role. Raffauf remained executive vice president and the search began for another new owner as Charlie wanted out. Running a sanctioning body did not turn out to be what he was led to believe. It became a tougher and tougher business to operate as time moved on.

To put a bow on the surreal events of that first day of Slater's ownership, when Silbermann returned to the IMSA offices after his encounter at the hotel with the new owner and Kelley, he got out of his car in the parking area. A horn honked. It was Mike Cone. Cone rolled down the window on his SUV, briefly thanked Silbermann for his work during the previous five years, said he was sorry, rolled the window back up, and then drove away.

leaving the door open to the overall victory by the Nissan.

In GTU, a bevy of factory-built Porsche 911 RSRs competed for the laurels won by the Heico team, which finished third and was one of seven entered from Germany and Switzerland. A Nissan Skyline GTR—an all-wheel-drive car designed for the FIA's Group A—was a notable entry, finishing tenth in class and twentieth overall.

At the 12 Hours of Sebring, the future of the WSC class was apparent when a Chevy-Spice, built in the shops of Mike Colucci and prepared by Gary Cummings and John Shapiro, chased the victorious Nissan 300ZX Turbo home. Bell, Wallace, and Weaver regularly exchanged the lead with Nissan drivers Millen, John Morton, and O'Connell. But shortly after sunset, a brake problem relegated the Chevy-Spice, entered by Morris Shirazi of the Auto Toy Store, to second. It was closely followed by the Mazda-Kudzu of Downing, McAdam, and Taylor.

The World Sports Cars hit full stride in the first sprint race at Road Atlanta in April. Four new Ferrari 333SPs and Mandeville's new Mazda-Hawk boosted the entry. In all, fifteen cars represented five engine brands and six chassis constructors. Eight new cars had started at the Rolex 24 at Daytona, ten started at Sebring, and fifteen at Road Atlanta.

Looking and sounding beautiful, the new Ferrari captured the WSC concept perfectly in its debut at Road Atlanta. Ferrari test driver Mauro Baldi came along to wring out the car for its first

Ferrari test driver Mauro Baldi transitioned to one of Scandia's 333SP entries. *Rick Dole*

competition. Baldi took the pole followed by his Eurosport teammate Jay Cochran. In the race, mechanical issues sidelined Baldi, leaving Cochran to take up the gauntlet and the victory. The Ferrari of Moretti and Eliseo Salazar finished second, and Wallace was third in the potent Auto Toy Store Chevy-Spice.

Moretti and Salazar won the next three races in the MOMO 333SP: the WSC-only sprint race at Lime Rock, the endurance event at Watkins Glen that combined all classes, and the sprint race at Indianapolis Raceway Park (IRP). IMSA had not raced at the IRP road course since the early 1970s and would not race there again after this event.

By June, new President Hal Kelley started leaning toward a technical rule change that would slow the Ferraris to help some of the team owners who were not getting the results they had expected. While attending Le Mans to help foster the inclusion of WSC cars at that twenty-four-hour race and elsewhere in Europe, Raffauf and Silbermann were reminded by Ferrari representatives of IMSA's written commitment from previous president Greenwood to not change the regulations in the first year of the WSC formula. It was decided there was no technical basis or demonstrated performance advantages to warrant a change to the rules. A variety of WSC cars had been competitive and the racing was close and entertaining.

Among those chasing the invariably red Ferraris, the Oldsmobile-Spice entered by Brix and sponsored by Motorola Phones proved to be very competitive. With no mid-season rule change, Dale won the last two events at Portland by seven seconds and the season finale at Phoenix by eleven seconds, trimphing over Moretti and Salazar in the MOMO 333SP.

Spaniard Vélez, on board the Scandia Motorsport 333SP, won the third leg of the West Coast swing at Laguna Seca. After a brief and difficult introduction at Sebring earlier in the year, actor Craig T. Nelson of TV's *Coach* fame returned to competition with his

Screaming Eagles team's Lexus V8-powered Spice at Laguna. Qualifying eighth and finishing ninth, he and co-driver Dan Clark recorded their best finish of the year as mechanical ills plagued the car at the remaining two events.

Taylor and Downing scored seven top five finishes and two eighth place finishes over the nine-race season to clinch the driver's championship for Taylor by three points over Dale, despite the Danka-backed entry failing to win a race. Due to its entries in the season-opening endurance races in the absence of Ferrari, Oldsmobile won the manufacturers title with three class wins. Ferrari, which had five wins spread over three teams, was beaten by four points. Mazda came third, only one point behind Ferrari.

It had been a very competitive freshman season for the new cars and for the teams campaigning them. The original WSC design was a success, and the fundamentals of the formula—such as open cockpits and flat-bottom chassis—would continue as a premier category for the next ten years.

## NISSAN DOMINATES GTS

With its GTS, GTO, and GTU classes, the Exxon Supreme GT Series championship remained as competitive as ever and was noticed around the world as a uniquely American product. Forays by IMSA into Japan and the Caribbean further confirmed the viability of the IMSA GT cars that were made from tube frames and silhouette bodies.

Behind the wheel of the 300ZX Turbos, Millen and O'Connell won an additional five races after Daytona and Sebring. Hoerr and Brassfield, driving the Uniden-backed Oldsmobile Cutlass, won three events.

The GTO class proved competitive for those racing in V8-powered American iron. Four drivers won from the schedule of seven sprint races. Joe Pezza claimed the championship in his pristine white Ford Mustang over Brian DeVries in an Oldsmobile and Charles Morgan in a Camaro.

In GTU, Leitzinger Racing dominated once again with the Nissan 240SX. Up-and-coming driver Jim Pace scored three wins to one by Peruvian Eduardo Dibos. Pace nipped Dibos by four points in the driver championship in a closely fought battle of consistent finishes all season long by both drivers. Auberlen won twice in the well-developed second-generation tube frame Mazda RX-7s. John O'Steen earned eight top five finishes out of nine races in one of the new Porsche RSRs, earning

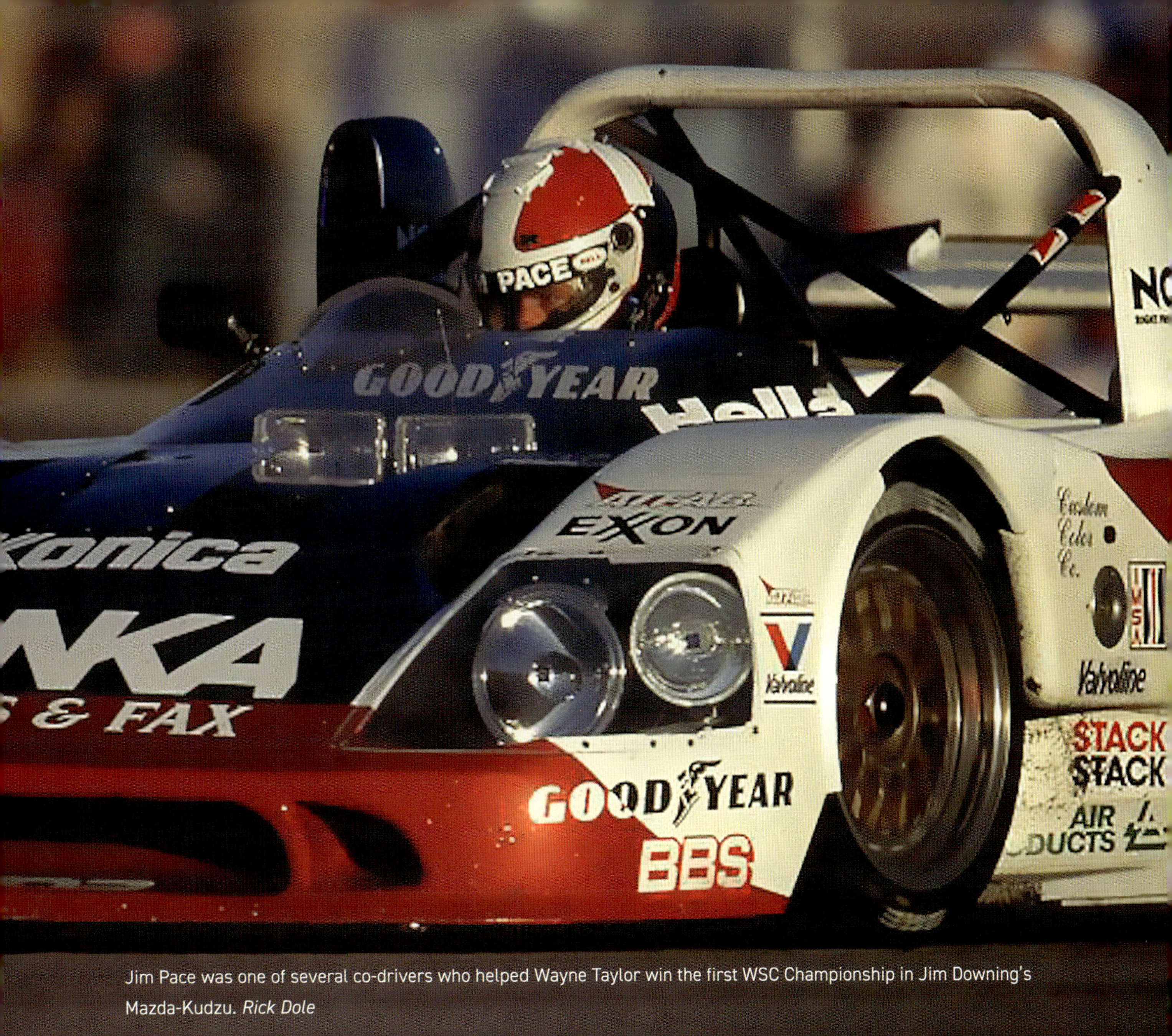


Jim Pace was one of several co-drivers who helped Wayne Taylor win the first WSC Championship in Jim Downing's Mazda-Kudzu. *Rick Dole*

third in the points battle. Nissan beat Mazda for the manufacturer crown by a mere ten points.

The supporting series continued to prosper. Significant growth in entries, manufacturers, and car variety in the Bridgestone Supercar Series led to a hard-fought title for David Donahue in Ed Arnold's BMW M5. Shawn Hendricks finished as the runner-up in a Nissan Stillen version of the 300ZX, ahead of Shane Lewis in a Corvette and Peter Farrell in the new Mazda RX-7 Turbo II. In addition, cars representing Lotus, Chevrolet, Pontiac, Ferrari, Porsche, Greenwood, and Saleen scored points during the year.

The Firestone Firehawk Endurance Series continued as the premier street stock racing program in North America. Trouble-free competition on shaved street Firestone Firehawk tires continued to mount in the record book, moving closer to one million miles of competition on street tires in the series.

A good view of the "office" in a World Sports Car. *Brian Cleary*

Grids regularly averaged from thirty-five to over sixty over the nine-race championship. It turned out to be the year of the Porsche 968. Numerous Porsche teams battled against equally numerous Pontiac Firebird teams in the Grand Sports class. Porsche won the manufacturer championship by six points.

Skip Barber Racing School driving instructor David Murry won the Grand Sport driver championship by finishing in the top four all but once and by winning the final three races in his red Porsche 968. The Sports category again showcased the ever-capable Honda Prelude, which won both the manufacturer and driver titles. An engineering coordinator for Honda, champion Forrest Granlund had been watching from the trackside fence only four years earlier. He went to the Skip Barber Racing School and secured the championship in his Honda Prelude V-TEC by one point over Farrell, who was driving his potent Mazda. Granlund won three times and was second four straight times in the eight-race series.

The Prelude Si was the car to beat in the Touring class, though they were chased all year by a fleet of Oldsmobile Achieva SC teams. Dave Daugherty clinched the championship and Honda added another manufacturer trophy to the display cases at American Honda in Southern California. There was an interesting 1994 "Rising Star" award winner—Tony George, president of Indianapolis Motor Speedway. He scored four podiums and one win at Road Atlanta co-driving with Andy Pilgrim in a Pontiac Firebird.

A wealth of future motorsports participants began their winning ways in the Barber Series. Diego Guzman, Juan Pablo Montoya, Mark Hotchkis, Jerry Nadeau, Jaki Scheckter, Divina Galica, Zak Brown, and Riccardo Donà competed during the season. Guzman, Hotchkis, Montoya, Nadeau, Luis Zervigon, and Hans De Graaff got at least one win each in a hotly contested open-wheel season of twelve races. After a consistent but winless season in 1993, Guzman's steady finishes brought him the title and the $100,000 career enhancement check at the end of the year. Many of the others would be heard from elsewhere in the future . . .

After the introduction of a major new prototype category with a new series title sponsor, IMSA racing was as strong as ever.

## "WE LOVED THIS CAR"

From Luca Pignacca

Luca Pignacca served at Dallara as the engineering liaison for the Ferrari 333SP. After working several years in Formula One, he accepted an offer to go to work at Dallara's headquarters, located in the small Italian town of Varano de' Melegari. When he arrived, the design and build of Ferrari's new WSC class sports prototype was just getting underway.

"This was my first design project at Dallara. I could stay in Formula One or go to Dallara. I chose Dallara as it was a shorter drive from home!

"They were finishing the design and the building of the first 333SP. Because I had the race experience and design experience as well, I became unofficially 'the guy.' Since the beginning I did problem fixing, reliability, spares, making sure that the parts were around.

"We built the first car. We received the engine from Ferrari and the Ferrari badge, to be put on the nose. Then someone from Ferrari came, we loaded the car on this trailer, and we went. So, I think that even chassis number one was built at Dallara.

The Ferrari 333SP was a game changer for IMSA, World Sports Cars, and international endurance racing. *Bill Tuttle*

"The chassis tubs were made at ATR, the first company in the world to build carbon composite monocoques for race cars and road cars, supercars.

"Mauro Rioli from the factory was doing a lot of the calculations as well of the carbon monocoque and helped to design the 333 monocoques, but it was codesigned by one of our guys who spent most of his time at Maranello. So, it was a codesign by Dallara and Ferrari. A whole team was involved, including Renzo Setti on the engine side and consultant Tony Southgate, who later engineered the car for customers at the racetrack.

"Suspensions, gearbox, and other systems were designed by Dallara in cooperation with Ferrari. The aerodynamics were done with 25 percent scale wind tunnel models at Dallara. The first wind tunnel was developed with the help of Giorgio Camaschella from Ferrari and Tony Southgate.

"Once customers had cars it was mostly Southgate and Rioli at the track. Sometimes we send a

The 333SP helped MOMO man Gianpiero Moretti bring a new outlook at Sebring, where his team won in 1998.
*Bill Tuttle*

The high-revving, sixty-valve iron block V12 was the power plant used in Ferrari's F50 road car. *Bill Tuttle*

couple of mechanics there, but we never supplied the real engineering support. Tony Southgate was the specialist, because Mr. Dallara has always been very practical and humble. He was not afraid to say, 'Hey, you know more than I do.'

"Southgate was unbelievable. He was really good. I think he spent a few months in Dallara. He gave us a lot of hints on suspension geometry, where things should be, weight distribution, all the little tricks that are very important, and if you do not know them, you don't make a good car.

"Mauro Baldi crashed the first car at Fiorano testing. I don't remember why, but he almost broke his leg because the 12-volt battery was not well fixed. I mean, the bolts to hold it down on the chassis were not strong enough. When he crashed, the battery came out and hit his leg. He was very lucky that it did not break.

"At Dallara, at the time, we used a lot of drawing boards because most of the design was by hand, by pencil. A few mechanical components were done by computing on very early 2D CAD. The bodywork was made by Dallara.

Ferrari was the only manufacturer in the World Sports Car category to build a "clean sheet" car to mate with its engine. *Bill Tuttle*

Renzo Setti, the Ferrari V12 guru, gained respect at Ferrari and worldwide for his work on the development of the 333SP engine. *IMSA Collection*

Tony Southgate, the engineering consultant for the Ferrari teams at the track, had a hand in the aerodynamics of the 333SP. *Rick Dole*

"When you make a carbon body, you must go for a pattern work. Then on top of it you build the mold, and then out of the mold you make the parts. The pattern work of the body was a big block of wood carved by hand by these incredibly talented guys. Fantastic guys! They carved it out of wood! We just gave them some contour sections every, I don't know, 200 millimeters maybe. They basically invented the shape of the body knowing that on this section, the contour was this one, on the next one, it was that.

"In 1995, there were significant bodywork changes. Using the original 25 percent scale model, and with a lot of help from Camaschella and Southgate, the result was more downforce and less drag, because the first nose was pretty blunt. A longer nose and side intakes were a lot slicker. We also added plexiglass panels at the cockpit sides to reduce drag and went to four headlights to improve lighting for nighttime races in IMSA.

"It was a simple car. The carbon monocoque was very basic, both shape and lay-up type. Everyone in Dallara, including Mr. Dallara of course, have very good remembrances of this car. We loved this car."

Scandia brought Ferrari the driver's title of the Exxon World Sports Car Championship in 1996 with Spaniard Fermín Vélez. *Bill Tuttle*

Like a scarlet ribbon, the Ferraris of MOMO, Lista, and Axiom hustled through the Corkscrew at Laguna Seca.
*Rick Dole*

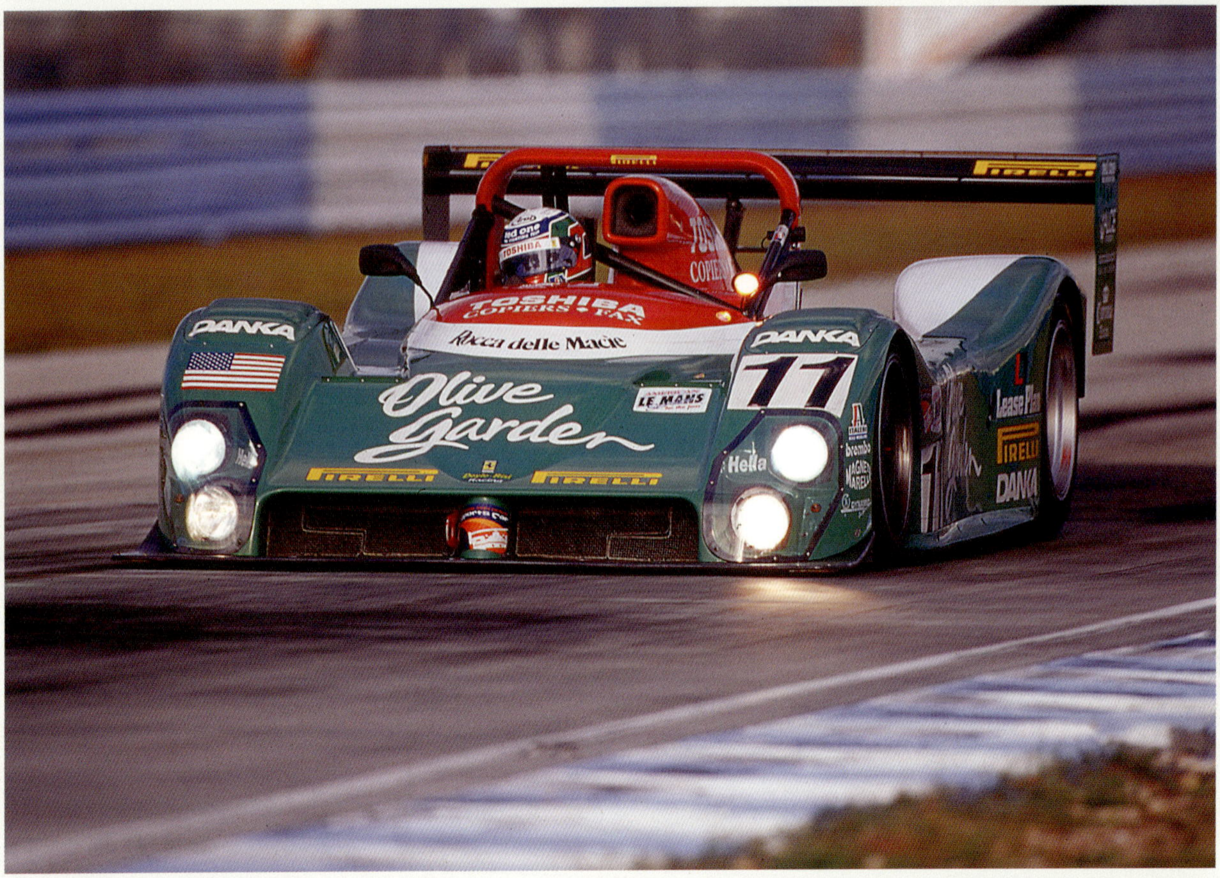

Ferraris began carrying Wayne Taylor to WSC victories following his championship stint in a Mazda-Kudzu. *Rick Dole*

Tony Ave flew the factory yellow Ferrari colors at Sebring in 1999. *Bill Tuttle*

## THE RILEY & SCOTT MK III

From Rob Dyson

Rob Dyson, one of the race-winning team owners with a Porsche 962 during the Camel GTP era, continued in the new Exxon World Sports Car class. After one season with a Ferrari-powered Spice, Dyson Racing became the first to race the Riley & Scott MK III. The MK III went on to become one of the most reliable and winningest cars in IMSA history and a regular rival to the Ferrari 333SP.

"For the World Sports Cars, IMSA had gone back to a rule book where private industry in the US and individuals could construct and build their own cars. Engine options were based upon the horsepower and torque of a five-liter American stock block V8.

"The engine had to be based on a production engine the way I read the rules. I saw that the 348 Ferrari had a nice three-liter engine. I told one of the guys to call a junkyard and get us one of them. I talked to Ted Wenz, an engine builder on Long Island. We got a couple of junkyard engines and took them apart, looked at them. What we found was good enough for me.

"Then we had to figure out what kind of chassis to put in it. Lola did not have anything. Our guys went over to England and Spice. I was always impressed that the Spice cars were very fast in GTP. They seemed to have had a nice suspension system in the front and something in the back that worked well with a variety of powerplants.

"Unbeknownst to us, Spice was going out of business! The car that we received did not have the

A stock block Ferrari V8 powered Dyson Racing's first WSC car. The lighter weight Spice chassis was quick, but the team could not pull off a win. *Randy McKee*

front suspension system we had seen in GTP. The springs and shocks were a conventional suspension completely different than what I was planning on. It was decided to see what we could do, and [we] headed to Daytona in 1994. The car was not bad but was not great. Because the engine was eight cylinders into two exhaust headers, we eventually decided it sounded better than the V12s in the new Ferrari 333SP.

"By the time we got to May in Lime Rock, and later Indianapolis Raceway Park, we were on the front row of the grid and right there with the 333SP. We made it work, but it was just a tough, tough situation. One of the reasons why we picked that Ferrari engine was it was small and light. I had thought the rule book meant street engines, not street-derived engines. Others were running aftermarket V8 engines with aluminum blocks, heads, etc. They were real racing engines compared to the little Ferrari.

"My longtime GTP crew chief and team manager Pat Smith rejoined the team in mid-season in 1994. Once on board again, he decreed, 'We need something bigger.'

"Dyson Racing became the first customer for the R&S MK III. We got the car at the end of 1994 and then we showed up at Daytona for the twenty-four hour in 1995. I took it out on the banking and said to myself, 'This car is absolutely terrific.'

"The Ford engine expired twenty minutes into the Daytona twenty-four hour. We needed somebody that knew how to build these fuel-injected Ford V8s. That's what led us to working with Mike and Benny Lozano. When we got to Road Atlanta that year, that's when the whole deal took off. There were a number of Ferraris, the very competitive Spice entered by Harry Brix, and us. We began a winning relationship with the Lozano Brothers that went on for eight seasons!"

The brain trust at Dyson Racing included crew chief Pat Smith, James Weaver, and Rob Dyson. Dyson's victory total in IMSA prototypes during the 1990s was unsurpassed. *Rick Dole*

Poughkeepsie-based Dyson Racing had many of the same crew members working together over the years, which was one reason behind its success. *Rick Dole*

2
GTE
Mobilnet
MOTOROLA
Cellular Phones
Snap-on
GOOD YEAR

CHAPTER SIX

# 1995: WSC HITS FULL SPEED

Ferrari's participation helped galvanize other race car builders who were considering the World Sports Cars. As the 1995 season approached, two distinctive new prototypes were being prepared to compete against Italy's most prominent racing marque. Scheduled to launch at the Rolex 24 at Daytona, both cars would play a prominent role in endurance racing, although their scripts for success followed very different paths.

When equipped with a Ford V8 and entered by Dyson Racing, the Riley & Scott MK III quickly became the American half of "Ford versus Ferrari," a battle that was sustained for the remainder of the 1990s. The majority of World Sports Car victories in the 1990s were recorded by Ford-powered MK IIIs or the Ferrari 333SP.

When it came to winning percentage, a second new car, the TWR Porsche, went on to become the most successful prototype carrying a Porsche engine in the company's history. The TWR Porsche won twice at Le Mans—each time it was entered—but a disagreement over rules when it came to contesting the Rolex 24 meant the TWR Porsche's only entry on American soil did not come until the inaugural Petit Le Mans, four years after it was built.

To expand the possibilities for the category, the WSC regulations were subject to change in the class's second season. There would be rpm limits differentiating V6, V8, and V12 engines. A provision was included to review the formula at mid-season.

New rules specifically designed to generate more participation created the Le Mans WSC class. These regulations led to the American-based team of Tom Walkinshaw building its Porsche-powered car with a chassis originally raced as a Jaguar. The TWR Porsche was powered by a turbocharged Porsche drivetrain, legal for the special class and eligible to compete only in the long-distance races at Daytona, Sebring, and Le Mans.

Brix Racing secured the WSC class win in the season opener behind the victorious Kremer Porsche. *Rick Dole*

But a preseason conflict ended up with Porsche withdrawing its new prototypes from Daytona's twenty-four hour following the early January test days. A disagreement arose when IMSA adjusted its technical specifications that were intended to competitively balance the regular WSC cars, which would campaign the entire season, and the Le Mans WSC entries. Deferring to IMSA's committed teams, which did not use turbocharging, IMSA stuck to its belief of what the technical balance should be. When the adjustment was made, Porsche saw the rules differently and withdrew from Daytona's season opener.

Despite the factory's absence, a Porsche won the Rolex 24. Privateers Manfred and Erwin Kremer were victorious with their older Porsche 962 that they had modified to the required open-cockpit configuration. An in-house Kremer Brothers creation,

After the withdrawal of the Porsche factory team due to disagreements over rules, the Kremer Porsche K8 won the Rolex 24 using the disputed WSC LM class regulations. *Lee Self*

Wayne Taylor shared Gianpiero Moretti's MOMO Ferrari while making plans to start his own team the following season.
*Rick Dole*

Jack Roush returned to Daytona with seventy-year-old Paul Newman, who co-drove to victory in GTS-1 with Tommy Kendall and Mike Brockman. *Lee Self*

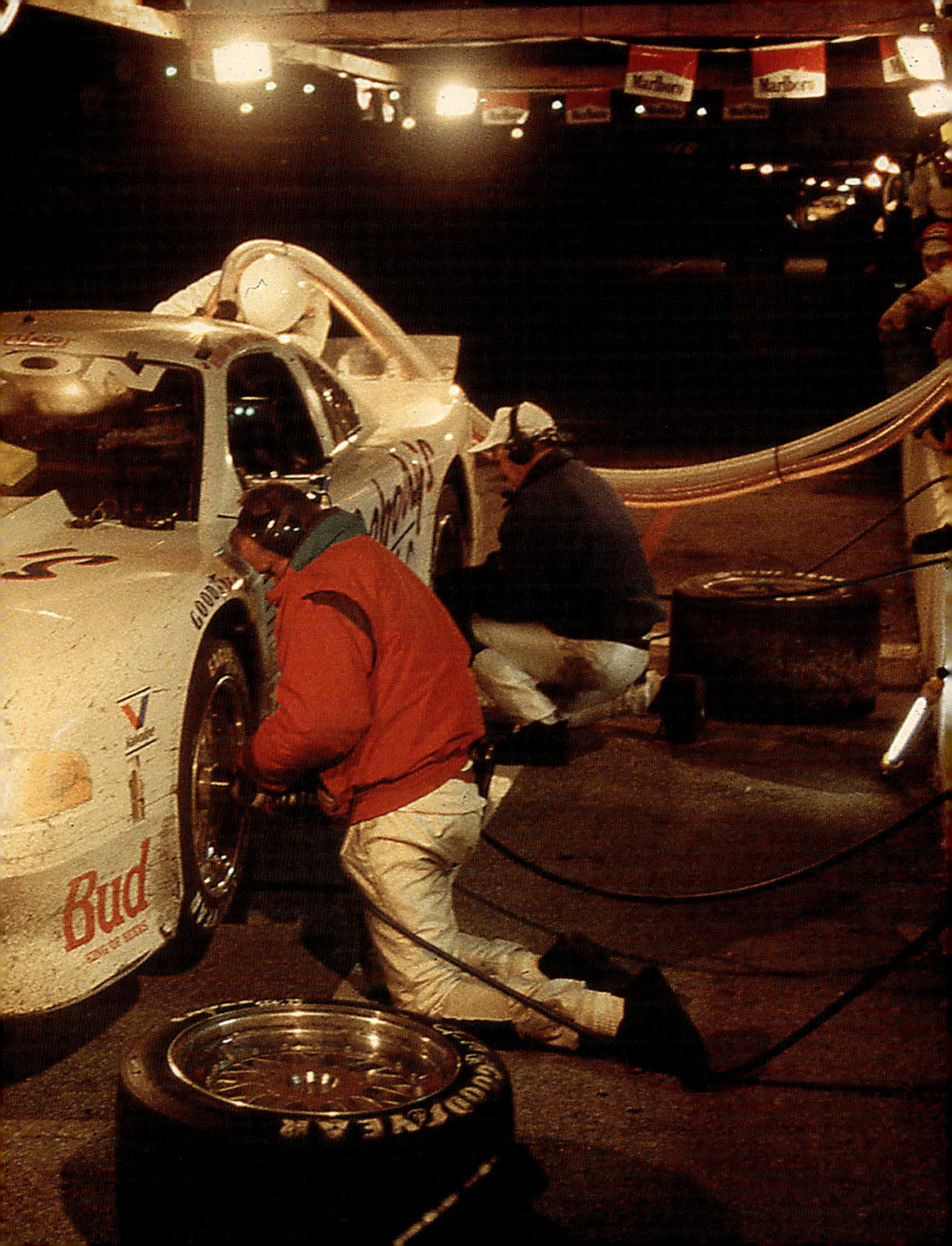
Marlboro
Bud

The Riley & Scott MK III-Ford of Dyson Racing led the pack through the esses at Road Atlanta. *Rick Dole*

The Scandia Motorsport team of owner Andy Evans (right) took Fermín Vélez to the WSC driver championship and Ferrari to the manufacturer title. *Rick Dole*

The exotic all-wheel-drive Bugatti EB110 that competed in IMSA was the only racing version ever made. *IMSA Collection*

the K8 won using the same IMSA turbo engine specifications that had led Porsche's factory officials to withdraw the TWR Porsche.

The twenty-four hour was the first true endurance race test for many of the WSC cars, and most faltered for a variety of reasons, which enabled the Kremer Porsche to win by being steady and reliable. The first entry by Dyson Racing with the Riley & Scott MK III fell out with a blown Ford V8 in the first hour. The Ferraris succumbed to engine problems as well, and only one was able to continue to the finish, opening the door for the Spyder K8 driven by Jürgen Lässig, Christophe Bouchut, Giovanni Lavaggi, and Marco Werner. Nineteen WSC and LMWSC cars started the race with seventy-four entries taking the green flag, making it one of the largest fields in Rolex 24 history.

## THE WSC CAR THAT GOT AWAY

By Martin Raffauf

The TWR Porsche originated in discussions between Max Welti, director of racing for Porsche AG; Tony Dowe, who had directed Tom Walkinshaw Racing's Jaguar program in GTP; and Alwin Springer, president of Porsche Motorsport North America. Some private brainstorming resulted in pitching Porsche's executives on entering the Le Mans World Sports Car category with a Jaguar chassis.

This joint project between Porsche and TWR started with an XJR-14 that was conceived for Group C and later used in GTP. Importantly, the car could be quickly completed by installing Porsche running gear into a modified version of the Jaguar. The roof was cut off the XJR-14 chassis while waiting for a decision by Porsche executives before installing a 3.0-liter Porsche flat six twin turbo.

The Formula One concepts behind the Jaguar XJR-14 made it one of the quickest cars in1992, but mechanical failures prevented Davy Jones from winning Camel's championship money. *Peter Gloede*

The goal was to run Daytona, Sebring, and Le Mans in 1995. Work had to be completed in the second half of 1994 so the car would be ready for testing prior to the Rolex 24. Initially, the project proved a hard sell at Porsche. As discussions proceeded, Springer provided an engine and transmission on loan during the build at TWR's Valparaiso, Indiana, facility.

Once confirmation was established at Porsche, the collaboration continued, and two cars were finished in December and entered for Daytona's twenty-four-hour race. The new prototypes were first taken to Charlotte Motor Speedway for a quick shakedown prior to the IMSA's prerace test at Daytona the first week in January. Porsche had signed Mario Andretti and his son Michael, Hans Stuck, Thierry Boutsen, Geoff Brabham, and Scott Goodyear to do the driving.

Springer reported that drivers complained about the handling during the Charlotte test. The front end wandered while the car was on the banking. Porsche engineer Norbert Singer realized that more wind tunnel testing was needed, but there was no time for that. He came to the rescue with a quick fix: a wing change to at least balance the car, reducing drag in the process.

Upon arriving at IMSA's test days at Daytona, the TWR Porsches turned laps two or three seconds per lap slower than the Ferrari 333SP on the combined infield and oval circuit. Ferrari officials and teams claimed Porsche was sandbagging with its new car. Porsche complained that the Ferrari teams were sandbagging, but they were two to three seconds a lap quicker, nevertheless. Having debuted the 333SP

The conversion to an open-topped WSC car gets underway at the TWR workshops in Valparaiso, Indiana.
*Tony Dowe / TWR Racing*

Converting from a normally aspirated V8 to a flat six turbo took some experimentation and a new gearbox case. *Tony Dowe / TWR Racing*

Reinforcing the roll-over structure was a necessary modification to the XJR-14. *Tony Dowe / TWR Racing*

Mario Andretti tested the new Porsche at the Charlotte Motor Speedway in late 1994. *Rick Dole*

TWR Porsche arrived in an era when most of a sports car's switches were still on the dash—not the steering wheel! *Tony Dowe / TWR Racing*

midway in 1994, Ferraris had not been entered in the Rolex 24, which meant there was no prior history of what the car could do on the Daytona track.

Ferrari officials and others complained to IMSA. The Italian firm had been given a written commitment by IMSA that no turbos would be allowed, and no rule changes would be made to WSC in the first year of competition by the 333SP.

But when looking ahead to the second season of WSC, Porsche had been given an OK for its plans for a turbocharged entry by IMSA President Hal Kelley. That agreement was made in a late 1994 meeting in Reno, Nevada, which included Mark Raffauf, Springer, and Porsche Competition Director Herbert Ampferer. Wary of introducing turbocharging to WSC, IMSA officials included a caveat that allowed for additional rule adjustments on the Porsche. Following the Daytona test, IMSA did some internal review of documents and the data collected at the track, and the rules were adjusted for the TWR Porsche. The air restrictors used to equate the engine to the atmospheric power plants in WSC were reduced by 2.5 millimeters, boost was fixed at one bar, and one hundred pounds were added to the minimum weight.

The rule changes were not well received at Porsche. Two weeks before the Rolex 24, Porsche CEO Wendelin Wiedeking made the decision to pull the plug and withdraw the cars from Daytona. Negotiations between TWR and Porsche in early 1995 resulted in the TWR Porsches being shipped to Weissach, the company's racing headquarters in Germany. They were parked in a corner of the basement.

By early 1996, team owner Reinhold Joest, who had followed the TWR Porsche project with some

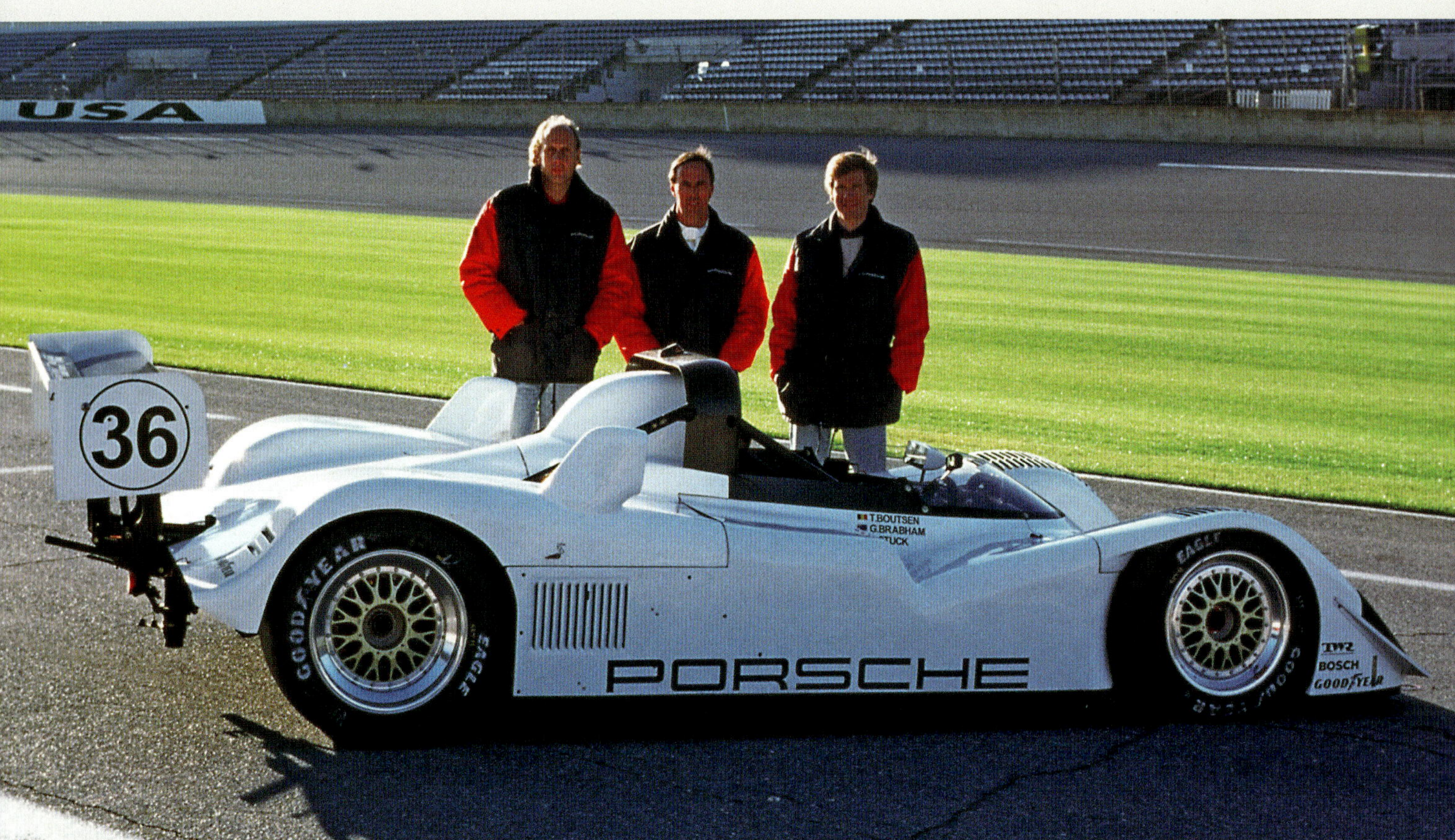


Intended co-drivers (from left) Hans Stuck, Geoff Brabham, and Thierry Boutsen standing with one of the two cars presented in January 1995. *Porsche AG Archive*

The TWR Porsche owned by Reinhold Joest returned to the US for its final race, finishing second in the inaugural Petit Le Mans at Road Atlanta. *IMSA Archive*

interest from afar, asked Porsche to let him have the cars to run at Le Mans. Porsche agreed. Some wind tunnel work was completed as well as testing.

Although its sister entry fell out due to a broken drive shaft, the No. 7 TWR Porsche ran faultlessly and won the 24 Hours of Le Mans by one lap over the factory GT1 Porsches that were powered by a newer water-cooled flat six turbo, a precursor to putting it into road cars. The "IMSA WSC" car had proven successful on the world's biggest sports car stage in its first race.

Joest had a deal from the factory to acquire the car if he won the race, and he duly took the No. 7 car back to his shops in Germany. The following year, Joest entered his lone WSC car while the factory focused heavily on its 911-based GT1 cars after a year of development. A race-long battle with the GT1 cars resulted in the TWR Porsche WSC winning again after a late fire caused the GT1 to drop out while leading.

At the end of 1998, the TWR Porsche ran its only race on American soil, the first Petit Le Mans, where it finished second to the Ferrari of Doyle-Risi Racing.

In just four entries, the car won Le Mans twice, had one DNF, and took second at the inaugural Petit Le Mans. The WSC car built from a Jaguar chassis and Porsche parts became an unqualified success after being parked in a basement. One of the TWR Porsches now sits in the Porsche Museum in Stuttgart, and the other resides in Joest's private collection in Wald-Michelbach, Germany.

## GTS-1 CLASS ARRIVES

The top-level GTS class gained a second category in 1995 beyond the IMSA-bred tube-frame chassis, which were no longer allowed to compete with turbocharged engines. The rules, designated as GTS-1, welcomed a new breed of production-based and factory-built race cars from Europe and Japan that were allowed turbos only if they were on the street vehicle. These regulations embraced IMSA's deep field of existing entries plus a new era of what were essentially factory-built street cars that could race effectively.

At Daytona, it was a tube-frame entry built by Roush Racing, a team long familiar with this type of engineering, that prevailed. On short notice, Jack Roush arrived with a Mustang numbered 70 in honor of actor Paul Newman, who had put together a last-minute sponsorship package to promote his new movie, *Nobody's Fool*. Sharing the Ford V8-powered car with veterans Tommy Kendall and Mike Brockman, the celebrated actor and longtime race competitor became the oldest winning driver in the history of the twenty-four-hour race. A Jochen Rohr–entered Porsche Turbo, one of the new production-based racers, finished a distant second.

The GT class for lighter chassis with less engine displacement, designated GTS-2, also included built-for-racing production cars. At Daytona, a race-long battle developed between the Bob Leitzinger Racing team's tube-frame Nissan and one of the new Porsche RSRs. The Leitzinger 240SX eventually lost by a lap to a quartet of European drivers. Finishing fifth overall, Lillian Bryner and Enzo Calderari were joined by Ulrich Richter and Renato Mastropietro in Victory Lane.

At Sebring's high-speed course with a variety of surfaces, and under alternately rainy and sunny conditions, the WSC category finally proved its endurance mettle by finishing first through fourth from a field of eighteen prototype starters. At the top was the Scandia Motorsport entry that brought Ferrari's 333SP its first endurance victory. Team owner Evans, Vélez, and Eric van de Poele earned a hard-fought win over the Auto Toy Store Chevy-Spice of established endurance racing pilots Bell, Wallace, and Jan Lammers, who finished on the same lap as the leaders along with the Kudzu DG-3 of Downing's team.

The Cunningham Nissan bounced back from Daytona to finish fifth overall and first in GTS-1 under power from its atmospheric V8, beating a Porsche 911 Turbo from Champion Racing and the Olds of Brix Motorsports. Hoerr won the pole in his Cutlass in the first outing for the new Aurora V8 engine, but over the long haul the veteran trio of Millen, O'Connell, and Morton were not to be denied in their well-sorted 300ZX chassis.

IMSA owner Slater scored the GTS-2 win with co-drivers Joe Cogbill and Auberlen. All the drivers were familiar IMSA competitors, and it was a popular result. Slater's 911 was entered by Alex Job and built by Dave Klym's Fabcar, who were also longtime IMSA participants who had helped sustain the tube frame category. Leitzinger racing was a close second once again, followed by Costa Rican Jorge Trejos and Dennis Aase in their Porsche RSR.

At least one rival team owner racing another manufacturer's car complained that the Porsches were given a break in the rules because Slater owned the series. "If the boss parks his car in the lot, it gets washed without anybody saying it needs to be done," said one of the team owners. But a majority of competitors appreciated Slater's participation, which kept him in touch with team owners' challenges, and the competition remained relatively close between all the manufacturers.

Slater's celebration at the twelve hours would be short-lived. The new World Sports Car and GT categories may have been hitting full stride with interest from teams, car builders, and fans, but behind the scenes, his ownership became problematic in just his second year when his handpicked president, Hal Kelley, sought to introduce a new business model for IMSA.

Fermín Vélez navigating the streets of New Orleans, where he clinched the driver's championship. *IMSA Collection*

During Cone's tenure, Kelley had tried to persuade the departed owner that IMSA should take control of all aspects of its events, including sponsorship, marketing, and all the other essentials that were usually handled by the promoter or track operator. At that time, it was decided IMSA did not have the resources in marketing, sales, and event operations to promote its own events. The new ownership was an opportunity for Kelley, who had advised Slater on his purchase of the sanctioning body, to give his concept another try, this time counting on Slater's resources.

This led to the announcement of several IMSA-managed events for the 1995 schedule. One at the Brainerd International Raceway was canceled, and a second at the Texas World Speedway would prove costly due to a poor turnout. There were revised contractual agreements for the Portland, Oregon, event and for other tracks. By April, Slater and his business advisor Dan White had enough of the negative feedback and difficult business arrangements launched by Kelley. He was let go at the Road Atlanta event, and veteran staffer George Silbermann was appointed the new president. Slater then started contemplating yet another sale of IMSA.

The Road Atlanta weekend was the scene of the first win by Dyson Racing's Ford-powered R&S

MK III in the hands of Weaver and, unfortunately, it was also remembered for two horrific accidents. One bad crash came early and one after the resulting long break and red flag.

While avoiding debris from an incident between two GTS-2 cars in the fast downhill of Turn Twelve, Fabrizio Barbazza's yellow Eurosport 333SP spun and rolled backward across the track. It came into the path of Jeremy Dale's Spice, resulting in a massive impact that seriously injured two drivers and destroyed two cars. The drivers survived due to the strength of the cars and the rapid medical response. Unfortunately, the incident curtailed the driving careers of Barbazza, who suffered a head injury, and Dale, who suffered extensive lower limb injuries.

A second serious accident at the bend on the back straightaway brought together the 333SP of Fredy Lienhard and Millen's 300ZX Turbo, both at full speed, sending them on wild rides with heavy impacts along the straightaway. One wheel broke free, careened up the embankment, and hit the side of a spectator's pickup truck, doing significant damage to the truck but luckily not injuring the two occupants.

Porsche's customer GT cars helped sustain the grids, including this very successful GTU class 911 of Larry Schumacher. *Rick Dole*

Leinhard got out of his car and walked back to the paddock before the medical team arrived. In a state of shock, he went to the airport and returned to his native Switzerland without stopping for any medical attention. IMSA officials followed up with him as soon as he arrived home. He admitted not remembering much from the accident or the trip back to Europe. He just remembered showing up at home, which indicated he had suffered a concussion.

Millen got out of his car, took off his helmet, and sat down on the embankment. Moments later medical personnel arrived, found symptoms they attributed to an injury, and sent him to the hospital after properly securing his head and neck. It would be his last race in 1995 due to a basal skull fracture, and the incident led to a significantly reduced Nissan program of five races for O'Connell in GTS-1.

On the positive side, Weaver's victory set the groundwork for "Ford vs. Ferrari." For the remainder of the season, the Dyson squad traded wins with the more numerous Ferrari entries, but they came up short in the championship after falling behind in the first two endurance races.

Vélez won three races and the title in Scandia's Ferrari. Taylor won twice at Lime Rock and Texas in the MOMO Ferrari, but it was an internally tumultuous year for the MOMO team, one where Moretti and Taylor did not always agree on race strategies. Weaver's five wins in the new MK III were not enough to overhaul Vélez's steady drives.

## BRIX OLDS LEADS GT

Nissan's reduced schedule brought to the fore the Brix Oldsmobile Cutlasses, one driven by Hoerr and Brassfield and the other by Charlie and Rob Morgan. The latter two co-drove to the win at Mosport, becoming IMSA's first victorious father-son combination. Hoerr, who won the final three GTS-1 races of the season, took home the championship. Brix Motorsports teammate Brassfield won twice. O'Connell won twice in solo drives during the remainder of Nissan's abbreviated season.

Stuck took two seconds and a third in his four appearances in the Champion Motorsports Porsche 911 Turbo in a partially factory-supported effort, which was the highest place of the cars new to GTS-1. The Bugatti EB110SC that was raced at Watkins Glen and Sonoma at Sears Point was a notable entrant. The striking silver all-wheel-drive supercar scored a fifth at the Glen and a sixth at Sears Point, marking one of the very few appearances of this car in competition anywhere in the world.

The onslaught of the race-ready Porsche RSR customer car bred a slew of new and returning competitors in GTS-2. BMW entered the fray with production-based M3s. The numerous tube-frame cars and production-based brands made GTS-2 a good fight all season long.

Costa Rican Trejos moved his program to the US from the FIA's Caribbean-based GT championship to partner with longtime Porsche expert Aase. After finishing third at Daytona, Trejos whittled away steady results to become the second Caribbean-based driver to win one of IMSA's GT titles, following in the footsteps of Dominican Luis Méndez's GTO title in 1980.

Auberlen's five wins out of the eleven races could not keep pace with Trejos's steady finishes and two wins. David Donahue and Paul Jr. were the primary drivers in the new BMW M3s and ran a strong partial season.

A new Canadian event, the Moosehead Grand Prix, proved dramatic and popular with fans. It was held at the Shearwater Naval Air Station in Halifax, Nova Scotia. Whenever a Royal Canadian Airforce C-130 had to land or take off, the air traffic control tower called IMSA race control. Racing activity was halted to let the big planes cross a section of the racetrack needed to get to one of the bigger runways. Fans and racers got an added side show, as well as views of a squadron of search and rescue helicopters based there, but IMSA would not be going back. The check from the organizers

Champion Porsche started its long run in IMSA with its stylish Porsche Turbo. *Rick Dole*

bounced after the event and IMSA, deciding not to pursue an international court process, never collected the balance due.

New Orleans returned with a new layout surrounding the Superdome. Weaver won the race, and Vélez—the winner at Halifax with Baldi—clinched his title at one of the more interesting temporary events (due to where it was and how it worked). The garage and paddock were on the floor of the Superdome. The Astroturf football field had been rolled up and race participants rolled in with haulers and equipment. The building provided a magnificent garage area, open to the public, and once the turnstiles were removed, access to the pits was right out the front door.

The supporting series menu changed in 1995. Gone were Barber Saab and the International Sedans. The first full season of the Ferrari Challenge for the identically prepared 348 and 355 models came under IMSA sanction. The cars were slightly stripped-down street machines with full roll cages and racing safety systems specifically prepared for track racing. Peter Sachs and George Robinson claimed the 355 and 348 titles, respectively, from a ten-race season. Other notable regulars in the first season were Derek Hill, Dr. Stephen Earle, Paul Frame, and Emil Assentato.

The Bridgestone Supercar Series included new venues on the streets of Long Beach and, uniquely, the Pikes Peak Hill Climb. Because of heavy snow on the traditional Fourth of July weekend, only half the Pikes Peak course could be used. Shawn Hendricks won on the mountain in an all-wheel-drive Dodge Stealth Turbo and claimed the series title after driving Ed Arnold's BMW M5s to four more wins in the nine-race season. Thirteen different manufacturers participated with high performance variants of their street products during the 1995 season, but unfortunately it was not enough for Bridgestone to continue backing the series.

The company's Firestone brand had already chosen to move on from sponsorship after 1994, instead focusing on expanding into the Indy Racing League and the Indy 500. The Firehawk Series had succeeded in revitalizing the reputation for the Firestone brand and its performance tires. The president of Bridgestone/Firestone flew over from Japan to one of the last events in 1994 to personally thank each of the IMSA staff and officials for the successful relationship and accomplishment of the company's goals. A very gracious thing to do. IMSA had delivered.

Previous International Sedan tire supplier Toyo stepped up and became the exclusive supplier of high-performance street radials to what became the IMSA Street Stock Endurance Championship. Veterans Pilgrim and Varde paired up in a Pontiac Firebird Formula, a pairing that carried Pilgrim to the Grand Sports class title. It was all Pontiac in Victory Lane except for one win by an RX-7 turbo.

Honda dominated the other three classes. Granlund captured the Sports title in a Prelude VTEC, John Green won the Touring trophy on board a Prelude Si, and Kris Skavnes took home the Compact class hardware in an Accord EX. The starting fields ranged between a low of fifty-one and a high of seventy-one entries.

The Slick 50 Pro Series was announced and added to the following year's schedule. It featured full-bodied and lightweight cars generally known as Sports 2000, which were branded as International Sports Racers. Joining them was the World Sports Racer, a similar Toyota-powered car made in Southern California.

James Weaver hustling his way to the win at the season-ending street race in New Orleans. *IMSA Collection*

## COMING TO AMERICA

From Fredy Lienhard

Swiss entrepreneur Fredy Lienhard took over the Lista line of office cabinetry and furniture business from his father. A longtime racer in Europe in a variety of single-seater and sports car categories, he came to IMSA in 1995 and remained a regular participant throughout the 1990s.

"After racing in Europe from 1966 to 1994, I wanted to make a dream come true and race in the US. I had been an entrepreneur with Lista in the US since 1970. I said to myself, 'Why not go for races as well?'

"Markus Hotz had the idea to buy a Ferrari 333SP, which would make it possible to join the IMSA Exxon World Sports Car championship. I got the car from Piero Ferrari himself at Fiorano in March of 1995. After a Swiss championship race in Hockenheim, which I won, we immediately sent the car to the US. I did not really think about how IMSA would work out—for me it was racing as I knew it to begin with. Very soon, I realized that there were quite a few differences.

Didier Theys behind the wheel of the impeccable Kevin Doran-prepared 333SP. Lista's Swiss brand industrial cabinetry was world famous for quality and style. *Rick Dole*

Fredy Lienhard and Didier Theys put their heads and driving skills together for five World Sports Car seasons. Later, Fredy Jr. drove in the Grand-Am with Theys. *Rick Dole*

"The first race at Road Atlanta was a disaster. The first impressions of the Atlanta [track] were breathtaking. It was all new to me and to my Swiss team HORAG. My laps were quite good, but luck was not on my side. The big accident I had in the race was completely unexpected—it just happened when I was lapping slower cars.

"I was very fortunate to escape with no injuries except some shock. It was hard for everybody, especially for my team and in the end, for my family

The Lista car at speed under Sebring's bright sun and the eye of a filtered lens. *Bill Tuttle*

members who were far away—no cell phones at that time!

"Despite this mishap, I felt that IMSA races were more than just racing. The spirit and the professionalism, the aim to give the spectators a good show, the fascination of the fans, and the high level of sportsmanship impressed me a lot. They were probably the reasons why I did not give up after this first race.

"Two months later, we started again in Lime Rock, a few miles from our US headquarters of Lista. With my experience from races in Europe, I knew that racing was a very good way to make our brand Lista better known. Lista had been very successful in

supplying racing teams. Even most of the Formula One teams used our cabinets. I always liked the idea of combining racing and business, a synergy of great importance.

"We repeated what we had done in Europe and very soon our brand was known better in the US. We invited customers and distributors to our races, which made them bigger fans for Lista. The personal relationships were developed better at the track than anywhere else. This was thanks to the common challenges in racing and business—sticking together in a competitive environment.

Didier Theys chasing the Ferrari of Wayne Taylor through the esses at Road Atlanta. Lista team owner Lienhard walked away from a big crash on his first trip to the track. *Rick Dole*

"I was very lucky to get to know Didier Theys. In the beginning, he was just a professional coach and the necessary second driver you needed to compete in endurance racing. But quite soon, he became much more—a real friend and mental coach. Without Didier, I could never have raced in the US.

"We raced together from 1995 to 2008, and even today we meet on track days in Europe. Our friendship helped me to cope with the challenges, which are quite heavy for a businessman-racer. But I learned a lot about coping with success and failures. That made me a better man—as a human being as well as a businessman."

Belgian driver Didier Theys scored several major sports car victories over the course of two decades in America, often in a Lista-backed car. *Rick Dole*

## THE FIRST CHAMPIONSHIP

From Wayne Taylor

"In 1994, I needed to either win races all the time or a championship. I decided a championship was better, because people do not forget. I joined up with Jim Downing and his three-rotor Mazda-Kudzu program. Jim gave me a car and co-drove. I'm sorry, but it was the ugliest race car I've ever driven. I didn't win a single race, but I won the first World Sports Car Championship.

"The Ferrari 333SP came out that first year of WSC with the Riley & Scott MK III still one season away from being on track. I decided I wanted to be in a Ferrari. I had spoken to Gianpiero Moretti of the

Wayne Taylor celebrating with co-driver Jim Pace and sons Jordan and Ricky in Victory Lane at Daytona. *NASCAR Archive and Research Center*

A second season with the Olds Aurora-powered R&S MK III was contested with co-driver Eric van de Poele. *Rick Dole*

MOMO squad already and we made a deal for 1995. I brought the money. I was adamant that I wanted to win races. We had a DNF at Daytona and then went to Sebring.

"It was always a difficult situation to decide who was going to start, Moretti or me. And so, there was a big race in Texas where there were hundreds and hundreds of people from my sponsors Danka and Konica. I said to Gianpiero, 'If you start, we are going to piss off the sponsors because you're going to go backwards.' I don't know where I had the balls to say these things. So, I suggested I would start and he would finish.

"Kelly Alvarado and all of the Danka people were there. We were leading or second to Michele Alboreto. I radioed to team manager Kevin Doran and said, 'Ask Gianpiero if I buy him a case of Wild Turkey, will he stay out of the car and let me do the whole race?' The answer was, 'No.' So I told Kevin I was not getting out of this car. I'm going to win this goddamn race. Tell Gianpiero he can have all the prize money.

"When it was time for the next pit stop, Moretti jumps over the wall, and I stay stuck in the seat. I said to Kevin on the radio, 'Put the fuel in, change the tires. I'm not getting out.' Off I went and won the race. When I came back, Moretti was gone. Pissed him off. But I got what I wanted and eventually got to know Alboreto really well and we became friends."

After one thousand miles, the Doyle-Risi Ferrari led the field home in the inaugural Petit Le Mans. *Rick Dole*

(From left) Emmanuel Collard, Wayne Taylor, and Eric van de Poele enjoying their win in the first Petit Le Mans. *Rick Dole*

Over three different decades, Wayne Taylor won in every IMSA prototype class—GTP, Camel Lights, WSC, and Daytona Prototype. *Rick Dole*

Bell Microproducts
EXON
90
43
Cystic Fibrosis Foundation
rain-x
16
EXON
Hella
BOSCH
PERRY ELLIS
ICE
SCANDIA
ALTA
3
MCI
EXXON
Konica
DANKA
Oldsmobile
30
momo

CHAPTER SEVEN

# 1996: CLOSE FINISHES HIGHLIGHT WSC

In the final hour on Sunday afternoon at the 1996 season-opening Rolex 24 at Daytona, Wayne Taylor was in agony. While behind the wheel of his Aurora V8-powered R&S MK III in the early morning, he had tried to maintain the lead despite slowing lap times due to a broken second gear.

Made sick by his driving efforts, Taylor gave way to young Scott Sharp, already a veteran road racing pro. When Taylor returned to the cockpit for the final stint, coming on strong behind him loomed the Ferrari of Max Papis, steadily gaining against the partially crippled leader in the infield portion of Daytona's high-banked track.

Taylor had left behind a Ferrari seat at Gianpiero Moretti's MOMO team and instead took his sponsor Doyle Racing to the Riley & Scott team. Driving for Taylor's former team, Papis was threatening to spoil the debut of the first Aurora-powered WSC entry and its four-valve V8 while trying to bring Ferrari its first win at the Rolex.

Former Formula One driver Papis was in MOMO's Ferrari sports car after deciding that moving to America would keep his career on the upswing. Given little time behind the wheel during the night, Papis was well rested when his team bolted on softer Yokohama tires, enabling him to post some of the race's fastest lap times and overtake Taylor for the race lead.

But there was a price to pay before the finish. Papis had to pit for fuel. His 120 miles per hour dash down the full length of Pit Lane to the MOMO team's stall helped earn him the nickname "Mad Max." The Riley & Scott team, which had calculated lap times and pit stops carefully but was gradually giving back its four-lap lead due to the broken gearbox, returned to the front and held on to win by sixty-five seconds.

In addition to a thrilling finish to the twenty-four hour, the number of teams representing a variety of manufacturer brands in WSC and GT

The WSC field took the green at Daytona, led by the two main protagonists. *NASCAR Archive and Research Center*

bode well for the series. The season opener also featured the C41 cars built by Yves Courage in France and two European-derived GT cars: the Callaway Corvette from Germany and the Lister Storm from the UK. The Dodge Viper brand was introduced for the first time in a major event competition.

On the racetrack, the 1996 season would be a stellar year for WSC, a mature formula where dynamic battles were often decided by slim margins of victory. But this did not translate into an increase in sponsors backing the sanctioning body, a problem that new owner Andy Evans, who bought the sanctioning body at the end of the season (detailed under subhead "Evans Buys IMSA"), would try to address the following year.

At the 12 Hours of Sebring, the Riley & Scott team prevailed once again. This time Taylor, Pace, and Eric van de Poele handled the driving. After winning the two major Florida endurance races back-to-back, the team's fans were chanting, "Le Mans! Le Mans!" in Victory Lane at Sebring, encouraging the team to add France's twenty-four-hour event to its schedule and attempt a sweep of

Wayne Taylor debuted the first R&S MK III powered by an Oldsmobile Aurora V8 in the Rolex 24. *NASCAR Archive and Research Center*

Reeves Callaway's Corvette finished third in GTS-1 at Daytona in its second year of IMSA competition. *Brian Cleary*

endurance racing's triple crown. Sponsor Doyle Racing, the Riley & Scott team, and manufacturers Oldsmobile and Pirelli elected to take up the challenge, but various misadventures brought the bid for endurance racing glory to an end. That didn't slow down the team's IMSA effort. Taylor and Pace won at the Texas World Speedway before Sharp rejoined Taylor at the Sears Point track in Sonoma, where the duo barely held off Papis and Moretti for the team's fourth victory of the season.

The Italian duo at MOMO won three times, taking home the laurels at Road Atlanta, Lime Rock, and Watkins Glen. The R&S MK III-Fords of Dyson Racing shined with WSC newcomer Butch Leitzinger behind the wheel. He won the final three races, co-driving with Paul Jr. at Mosport and Daytona with a solo victory at Dallas in between.

The four mid-season races run at Lime Rock, Watkins Glen, Sears Point, and Mosport were decided by a total of just five seconds. Papis caught Weaver with a pass in the grass on the last lap at Lime Rock to win by 0.572 seconds. At Watkins Glen, Papis ran down Taylor to win by 3.8 seconds. (Late race contact in Turn One between the two drivers had resulted in the Ferrari dropping nineteen seconds behind before a great comeback by Mad Max.) At Sears Point, Paul Jr. ran out of fuel on the next-to-last lap. Taylor, who had battled Papis the entire race nose to tail, this time pipped the Italian at the finish line by just 0.198 seconds.

Following these incredible finishes, the visit to Canada's high-speed Mosport circuit produced its own extraordinary last-lap result. With one lap to go, Papis dived past Paul Jr. to put his Ferrari into the lead. But in the last corner of the final lap, yards from the start/finish line, Paul Jr. would return the favor brilliantly in his R&S MK III, perhaps catching the Italian off guard. Overtaking on the inside at Turn Ten, Paul Jr. pulled off one of the cleanest and best-timed moves anyone had ever seen.

It was the first IMSA victory for Paul Jr. since his breakthrough Camel GT season in 1982. After the incredible finish, the two drivers congratulated each other and raved about the competitive fun, regardless of the outcome. Two world-class drivers, one remaking a name for himself in IMSA and the other making a name for himself in America, had put on the show of the decade. "The Pass" is still referred to by the Mosport faithful as one of the finest moves ever witnessed at that daunting Canadian circuit.

Taylor won his second WSC Championship in three years. This time he won four of the ten races, including the two big ones at Daytona and Sebring. Taylor's marketing prowess and relationship with Doyle Racing was working well on and off the track.

## HOERR, BRASSFIELD DUEL IN GTS-1

In GTS-1, Brix Motorsports and Oldsmobile dominated the GT show for most of the year. The Nissan 300ZX, the three-rotor Mazdas, and others were gone. New cars and more potent Porsche 911 Turbos were catching up but were not yet fully developed. Brix decided to give its GTS-1 defending champion, Hoerr, team manager responsibilities.

Typical Sunday morning issues. *Brian Cleary*

As the new team leader, Hoerr focused on helping to get his good friend and teammate Brassfield a title.

Co-driving often kept Brassfield and Hoerr close in the points. But this *Friends* episode resulted in Brassfield winning one solo race while Hoerr took two, which made the difference in the points title in favor of Hoerr. Several capable teams gave chase—Charles Morgan and son Rob on board an Olds Cutlass, Dibos in his Yokohama-shod Mustang, and Stuck and Bill Adam in the Evo version of the Porsche Turbo of Champion Racing.

The Morgans earned first-place points at Daytona in a temporary alliance with Brix, sharing the car with John Gooding and Joe Pezza. Brassfield and Hoerr pitched in with the front-running Aurora after their entry had caught fire, but they could not earn points.

Stuck and Adam prevailed in the Porsche Evo at Sebring. The Aurora then won every race except the season finale at Daytona, which Stu Hayner and Roger Schramm captured in the latter's Camaro.

Following the Cougar XR7 and Oldsmobile's Cutlass, the Aurora became the third American front-wheel-drive model to be developed into a 7/8ths car that was fully approved by IMSA. Like the first two, the conversion was well executed to the point that few in the paddock or grandstands noticed. The street car had a long wheelbase and short overhang, so the race car was shrunk to fit the regulatory template and converted to rear drive. The new 4.5-liter, four-valve Aurora V8 was then crammed into the engine bay.

GTS-2 witnessed continued growth from manufacturer-built customer racing cars from Porsche and BMW with a few of the better tube-frame cars remaining in the mix. Larry Schumacher won the championship in his 911 RSR. Team owner Milner's BMW M3s and Ecuadorian Henry Taleb, in the ex-Leitzinger Nissan 240SX car, scored victories as well. Javier Quiros, yet another convert from the FIA's Caribbean-based series, ran a limited season

A classic Daytona duel in the fog—the Ferrari of MOMO against the MK III of Riley & Scott. *Brian Cleary*

The Olds Aurora GT entries became the second "downsized" car created for the GTS-1 class. *Rick Dole*

in his Toyota before winning the finale at Daytona in an M3.

The IMSA Street Stock Endurance Championship stormed onward with starting fields averaging just under sixty cars for the ten-race series. Toyo provided outstanding tires to the four classes, where once again the championships were won by Pontiac and Honda drivers. But the title trophies for manufacturers went to Pontiac, Toyota, Honda, and Nissan, respectively, for the Grand Sports, Sports, Touring, and Compact classes.

The highlight of the year was a twenty-four-hour race at Mosport, where a Touring class Honda Prelude Si took the overall win. John Green, Terry Earwood, Mark Hein, Gary Blackman, Lance Stewart, and Kris Wilson peddled the car twice around the clock. The top GS class car finished eighth overall.

Diversity in Grand Sports put Pontiac Firebird Formulas into the winners' circle five times. Mustangs won three times and Mazda RX-7 Turbo IIs won twice. John Heinricy won the GS championship, proving to himself and his fellow GM engineers that their F-body performance Firebird was a winning package. Heinricy was well known for his driving, but he was probably better known for his ability to engineer production cars, such as the F-body Camaro and the Firebird.

The Ferrari Challenge entry grew after an increase in the number of Ferrari 355s. Dr. Stephen Earle won the championship and would become a mainstay in the series. Jim Kenton took the 348 Series crown over a growing list of entry-level drivers, some of whom would move up to other series.

The new Slick 50 Pro Series for Sports 2000 and Toyota sports racers provided up-and-coming drivers as well as experienced shoes with an economical race car and lots of close competition over the eight-race series. The first two champions in the inaugural year were Mike Davies in the Toyota World Sports Racer (WSR) and Alex Smith in the International Sports Racer (ISR), each claiming four wins in their respective categories. Over the course of the season, thirty-eight different drivers participated in the WSR group and twenty-three in the ISR group.

## EVANS BUYS IMSA

Since its inception, IMSA's business model had always been paddock driven—as evidenced by the number of participants in its entry level series. Income was primarily derived from membership licensing, race entry fees, and sanction fees from the racetracks. Sanction fees, which varied from event to event, represented what promoters were willing to pay to bring the IMSA "show" to their location. Although never ignored, in-house marketing was secondary. For example, when Lee Gardner moved to IMSA in the 1980s after working to promote the Camel GT for R. J. Reynolds, he was the first marketing person on the staff.

As a result of R. J. Reynolds's lucrative sponsorship and sports marketing expertise, IMSA was a motorsports competition platform that fulfilled the needs of corporate clients from its inception. Companies showcased their street tires through IMSA series title sponsorship, including Goodyear, BFGoodrich, Firestone, Bridgestone, and Toyo. Exxon, employment firm Kelly Services, Champion Spark Plug, Eastern Airlines, LuK Clutches, and others benefitted from their series sponsorships over the years under the Camel GT umbrella. In addition, the platform helped individual teams bring in sponsorship by companies promoting beer, oil, soda, restaurant chains, automotive components, and countless other products or services. They all rode the wave of promotion and activation that R. J. Reynolds provided to events from its large budget, a budget that disappeared after the 1993 season.

By 1996, all but one of IMSA's longstanding sponsors from the previous three years had also departed. Exxon remained, but most of the others had gone for various reasons, some related to IMSA, some not. This was the shadow cast while Charles Slater sought a new owner.

IMSA President Silbermann spent most of the summer shuttling between various suitors trying to buy the company. The staff at IMSA felt very loyal

Wayne Taylor celebrating in Victory Lane with sons Jordan and Ricky, who would return as winning drivers themselves. *NASCAR Archive and Research Center*

to Slater since he treated everyone well, respected IMSA's business, and listened. His acquisition had rescued IMSA from Cone's poor leadership, but Slater was not the right type of guy to run a sanctioning body, and he had come to realize this.

Late in the 1996 season, he sold the sanctioning body to team owner Evans. Because Evans was a single competitor in IMSA, unlike the other potential buyers that were composed of groups of racers, Slater considered it the best deal. The board of directors concurred it was best to avoid ownership by a group of competitors, which raised the specter of both infighting and self-serving decisions that favored only their interests. The principal of International Motor Sports Group (IMSG) and president of the Seattle-based Dominion Income Management Group, Evans had been a Camel Light and WSC team owner in IMSA for several years and was expanding into the new Indy Racing League and the Indy 500.

Evans's successful business background and strong connections in the sports marketing world were considered a positive. He had an association with Bill Gates of Microsoft, whose stock sales were organized by Evans's company on Wall Street. He seemed a reasonable choice for the future of IMSA.

Evans had brought new and interesting sponsorships to IMSA already, but he was quirky and he surrounded himself with both good and bad people. Unfortunately, it always took a while to figure out which ones were the good ones. He had a vision for sports car endurance racing and how it could be marketed. He set high expectations, but the results were well below those expectations. Evans's off-the-cuff dictatorial style and the people he brought in to oversee and direct IMSA led to the departure of most of the remaining veteran IMSA staffers within the first year of his ownership.

A hard-fought maiden win for car and team.
*Brian Cleary*

## THE MK III MAKES ITS MARK

From Bill Riley

Bill Riley worked with his father Bob to design the fast and successful Intrepid GTP. Bob Riley and Mark Scott subsequently formed Riley & Scott with headquarters in Indianapolis, where the main task was building tube-frame Trans-Am cars. Once it was decided to build a new WSC prototype, Bob Riley designed the Riley & Scott MK III using Computational Fluid Dynamics (CFD). Bill Riley, often working as a chassis consultant with outside teams, including NASCAR teams, worked with his father in all phases of what became one of Bob Riley's signature cars.

"WSC looked like it was something we could build in our shop with our tools. We didn't have an autoclave, so we couldn't do a carbon tub. From a design perspective, we believe this was the first race car designed totally with Computational Fluid Dynamics,

One of America's most successful race car designers, Bob Riley considered the MK III one of his best. *Rick Dole*

which was new then. CFD, as it was called, was a computer program that helped designers map virtually every square inch of a car's design to determine how the air flow over the body would work at racing speeds.

"The first two cars were made of aluminum tubing with stressed carbon skin. One of our fabricators found numerous issues with cracking and was able to break sections in a press. So we scrapped those and went to steel tubing.

"We went to University of Michigan with a model that had a teardrop body to do some wind tunnel work. It was a bit of a sad run. For aerodynamics, slab sides worked better, but they just did not look as cool! It would have been nice to have a teardrop car, but the air wanted to go straight. We played with the nose angle and everything else. But the original layout with the wedge nose and the general layout all became part of the car. It was just the sides that we changed.

An Olds Aurora V8 powered the 1996 victory at Daytona by the Riley & Scott team with drivers Wayne Taylor, Scott Sharp, and Jim Pace. *Rick Dole*

The Dyson Racing "twins"—numbers 16 and 20—won races and championships over the course of eight seasons in IMSA, the USRRC, and Grand-Am. *Rick Dole*

"Rob Dyson became our first customer. We tested briefly at Roebling Road near Savannah prior to the twenty-four hours in 1995. I remember one funny story from that first test. James Weaver had driven it and was talking about the car. He said it did not feel good. Thought it was slow.

"My dad grabbed me to go out and watch the car on the track. We went to the back side of Roebling Road and the car was dynamite. It didn't do anything goofy. It just looked right. We came back to the pits, and I remember Weaver kind of complaining, nothing horrible but constructive complaints.

"James finally went to team manager and crew chief Pat Smith and asked, 'What kind of times did they run at Savannah previously in the Porsche 962?' Pat always kept complete notes on everything. He discovered the new car was two seconds quicker on the lap times than the Porsche. Weaver looked at my father and says, 'I think we're going to be OK. Yeah, I think we're going to be OK.'

"They only change on the car was a switch from a Ford Mustang steering unit. It was simple to mount and designed for racing but did not work well. After changing to engines built by the Lozano Brothers, the car won in its third time out at Road Atlanta and interest grew.

"For 1996, Wayne Taylor and his sponsor Danka came around and ordered a car to be fit with the new Oldsmobile four-valve Aurora V8 engine. It won both Daytona and Sebring that year, and more orders started coming from a variety of customers using Chevy, Lexus, and BMW V8 engines, and Judd racing engines in Europe.

"Once Oldsmobile and Pirelli got involved, and after winning Daytona and Sebring, we made a last-minute decision to go to Le Mans in 1996. We had to run an air-restricted engine under the ACO regulations for Le Mans as opposed to an rpm-limited version in IMSA. The Aurora V8 was never developed for that, and we also had to change fuel to their lower quality spec. There just was not enough time to do it all right.

"Oldsmobile did work hard to get to the best engine we could have. We needed a cylinder head with smaller ports and all the other stuff that goes with it. We changed to a shorter splitter in the front,

Wayne Taylor switched to the red paint scheme of sponsor Toshiba in 1997, his second year onboard a R&S MK III.
*Rick Dole*

The MK III accommodated a range of engines—a Judd V-10 in the case of Gabriele Rafanelli's entry. Other power plants came from Ford, Chevrolet, Oldsmobile, Lexus, and BMW. *Rick Dole*

a smaller rear wing, and some fender covers and a bunch of little stuff to streamline it up.

"We went to the pre-qualifying and qualified third with it, because you could get a clear shot through the Porsche curves. There were people coming up to me saying no car has ever been through the Porsche curves like that. But in the race, you couldn't gain time there because of traffic. The race just went to shit right off the bat.

"On the first pit stop, I came the closest I have come to death at a race. We had hired a transporter truck from Pacific Formula One Team and a couple of their guys to help us out. We gave them a list of stuff that they had to do. One thing on the list was nitrogen bottles for all the air guns.

"When the car comes in for the first stop, we rattle the wheels off, put the wheels back on, and one of the crew guys hits the trigger on the air gun. Smoke starts coming out of it, like black smoke coming out of a broken aircraft engine. Then suddenly, a huge explosion and the regulator blows off the metal canister where the air gun is connected. A big ball of flame comes out around the canister and into the pit area.

"We dropped the car off the jack, Scott Sharp leaves, and we all ran away. There were air hoses flying all over the place, burning gas of some sort. It was just a disaster. Big Greg Eliff, our gearbox guy, saunters over and starts turning the nozzle on the canister off. The guys from Pacific Formula One ordered oxygen rather than nitrogen. Nice. It destroyed all the guns and now we had no nitrogen. Luckily, our IMSA friend Charlie Cook was there with a Viper and he lent us a bunch of stuff. This was during the race and everything had to be done before the next pit stop.

"Things continued to go wrong. We were on the wrong brake pads. We were going through brake pads. Jim Pace had a bad off. It was just one thing after another.

"I think we built a total of twenty-six MK IIIs. My dad said the car hit all the marks right off. It was the right car for the market for the right price and a car that team owners knew was competitive. Without an engine, it cost $245,000—a very good deal."

Team owner Henry Camferdam deployed a Ford-powered R&S MK III during the 1999 season. *Rick Dole*

## THE STAR CHAMBER

By George Silbermann

The Star Chamber may or may not have existed.

Within the massive infrastructure of the Houston-based Exxon Corporation, the story goes, there was a top-secret division, where select young executives might be assigned if they showed "the right stuff" early in their climb up the corporate ladder. One version of this tale involves short-term assignments to an isolated, dedicated, internal think tank charged with using advanced algorithms and data collected from sources around the globe to predict gasoline and petroleum product pricing two to three years into the future, or even further.

IMSA had been accustomed to dealing with major corporations in the sport from the beginning. This included entitlement sponsors such as R. J. Reynolds, Bridgestone, and others. IMSA also enjoyed strong relationships with many other major companies who were involved in the sport in a variety of roles.

Perennial Fortune 500 powerhouse Exxon was unlike any series sponsor IMSA had ever worked with before. It was the embodiment of Big Oil and a unique corporate world unto itself. Exxon had a very conservative culture and an even more conservative approach to business, but it was also unafraid to step outside the box and take calculated risks. The involvement with IMSA represented both dimensions. Yes, traditional metrics like return on investment drove the business relationship with IMSA, but corporate officials also saw a unique opportunity. They believed the timing was right and took on major title sponsorship of the GT Series and then added the World Sports Car Championship to the portfolio.

A budding young Exxon executive named Alan Jackson was assigned as Exxon's point person. He quickly learned about, and acclimated to, the unique world of racing and IMSA. Jackson brought a new perspective, much like the R. J. Reynolds managers who had helped shape the sport in positive ways during the preceding decades.

Exxon supported racing series in traditional ways and in areas where a tobacco company was prohibited by law, such as television spots. Some of this support was extremely creative and innovative. Exxon, for example, would occasionally run series-specific advertising that only appeared in print once, which would eventually become sought-after collector items.

The timing was right for Exxon and IMSA, but not in all respects. When the relationship began, Exxon was already chafing under the huge financial strain of the 1989 Exxon Valdez oil spill in Alaska. This would continue to have an effect for many years to come. Exxon's relationship with IMSA corresponded to financial strife in the US economy as well.

After seven years, Exxon concluded its relationship with IMSA at the end of the 1997 season. The following year, Exxon and Mobil announced a $73.7 billion merger, forming a new company called ExxonMobil. The largest corporate merger at the time, clearly this had been in the works for some time behind the scenes and, no doubt, had a bearing on many of Exxon's non-petroleum endeavors, like IMSA.

In time, Exxon's senior management became dissatisfied, as they hoped the Exxon World Sports Car Championship would achieve the same level of interest as the preceding Camel GT Series in only a handful of years. Candid conversations also acknowledged that Exxon's leadership was uneasy about the turmoil following a series of ownership and management changes at IMSA in a relatively short time span.

As the relationship between Exxon and IMSA began to wane, Alan Jackson was transferred elsewhere. The story goes that he was reassigned to the Star Chamber. This was never confirmed or denied.

EXXON
EXXON
RÖHR

CHAPTER EIGHT

# 1997: A PSR SEASON FULL OF CHANGE

One of Andy Evans's first missions as the new owner was to convert IMSA into a marketing company. Throughout 1997, the marketing staff was expanded, new departments like IMSA properties, business development, account services were added, and staff members were hired to work as liaisons to manufacturers. Though the intent had merit, none of these efforts succeeded in generating new sponsorship for the sanctioning body. Fortunately, Exxon remained as the series title sponsor for both the World Sports Cars and GT Series, which provided stability.

Evans's approach was a radical step away from the IMSA model that had been successful for almost three decades. This model had survived two earlier owners in the 1990s, in part because the staff established under founder Bishop had remained largely intact. But Vice President Mark Raffauf, the longest tenured employee in IMSA, chose to depart in November 1996, not wanting to continue down the path set by the new owner. "Evans looked like a crook and acted like a crook," said Raffauf. Evans was, in fact, a crook, according to a March 1993 *Wall Street Journal* article that recounted his jail time for bank fraud.

Additional senior staff, including Silbermann, Don Schnieders, and others, also left prior to the onset of the main 1997 event schedule.

As part of the new marketing approach, Evans and his advisors rebranded IMSA, abandoning nearly three decades of motorsports history and the legacy associated with the original IMSA logo designed by Bishop. Though the logo ownership was retained, it was kept behind the scenes well into the 2000s before being brought back. The new name under Evans became Professional SportsCar Racing, or PSR. (Some of the more cynical racers began referring to PSR as "pisser.") Its logo looked

The Porsche 911 GT1 of Jochen Rohr's team and the GTR-1 of Panoz Racing battled one another throughout the season. *Rick Dole*

surprisingly like that of the Indy Racing League and even used the same colors.

Beyond internal changes to convert IMSA into a marketing company, Evans generated a lot of media publicity by calling for another paradigm shift. He regularly made proclamations about rules that would give GT cars equal emphasis and lap times as the World Sports Cars, a significant shift away from having prototypes as the lead category that was first established during the GTP era of the 1980s and then followed by WSC in the 1990s. He went as far as establishing an office in Le Mans to maintain communications with the Automobile Club de l'Ouest (ACO) at Le Mans, which was embarking on a renewed focus on GT cars for its twenty-four hour.

The talk of change led to a record team turnout at the season-opening Rolex 24 at Daytona, where ninety-six cars were entered—the majority being GT cars—and eighty qualified for the race. Though the rules allowed for manufacturers' new unibody GT cars that were emerging in Europe to join the traditional IMSA tube-frame GT cars, the WSC prototypes remained fastest overall, absent any horsepower restrictions that had been broached by Evans to create an equivalency.

In a garage discussion prior to the twenty-four hour, Elliott Forbes-Robinson and John Schneider convinced team owner and driver Dyson to run both of his Ford R&S MK. III cars for the entire race, the primary No. 16 and the backup No. 20. It turned out to be a prophetic decision. Originally, the plan was to start two cars before withdrawing one early—the No. 20 driven by Dyson, Forbes-Robinson, and Schneider. Instead, Paul Jr. was assigned to be the swingman, initially joining the

After winning at Daytona, Dyson Racing was ready to go at Sebring. *Bill Tuttle*

Different lighting strategies were deployed at Daytona, where visibility could be a challenge. Klaus Scheer's Porsche team spotted an advantage. *Brian Cleary*

No. 20 lineup before swapping over to share the No. 16 car with Weaver, Wallace, and Leitzinger.

Attempting back-to-back wins, Taylor and Doyle Racing returned with their Oldsmobile Aurora R&S MK III along with a second Aurora-powered entry run by Dibos Racing. Moretti's MOMO squad and Evans's Team Scandia carried the Ferrari banner. Three more R&S MK IIIs with various engine combinations, two Kudzus, Roger Mandeville's Hawk—which had been converted to Chevy V8 power—and a new French Courage helped fill out a seventeen-car WSC field.

Vélez started the Scandia Ferrari on the pole, but the No. 16 Dyson Racing R&S MK III set the pace and was leading until 9:00 p.m. when a valve train failure ground it to a halt. By this point, the No. 20 was already six laps behind the leaders. Overnight and into the early morning, Forbes-Robinson, Schneider, Dyson, and Paul Jr. drove around steadily, chipping away at the lead when those in front faltered with various mechanical woes. About two hours before dawn, the No. 20's Ford V8 began showing signs of overheating, but the nighttime temperatures helped keep it cool. Leitzinger was

Prototypes representing Chevrolet, Ferrari, Ford, Mazda, and Oldsmobile took the green at Sebring.
*Brian Cleary*

CHRYSLER
CHRYSLER
PROFESSIONAL SPORTSCAR RACING
Sportscar
EXXON
Superflo
EXXON
Superflo
EXXON
DANKA
TOSHIBA
TOSHIBA
DANKA
30
YOKOHAMA
Playpiso
momo
rain-X
16
16
SCANDIA
ACXIOM
TEAM SCANDIA
43

drafted into the lineup, and by daybreak he had the car in the lead despite the overheating issue.

When Weaver and Wallace returned from a restful night at their hotel, they too joined the No. 20 lineup. Crew chief Pat Smith and the host of drivers managed the car masterfully, especially Leitzinger, who drove the last stint with the car constantly puffing smoke. He finished one lap ahead of the Scandia Ferrari. The second Aurora-powered R&S MK III was seventeen laps back from the Ferrari.

An emotional Dyson earned his first Rolex 24 trophy and gold watch. The seven drivers represented the largest ever driving team in a winning car at Daytona. As was allowed at the time, drivers could move back and forth between team cars but could only earn championship points after a minimum specified amount of drive time in the first car driven. Only Forbes-Robinson drove sufficient time to earn points, which would become a significant factor later in the season.

## NEW CLASSES FOR GT

Following Evans's trial balloon of putting more emphasis on GT cars, PSR made a half step by accommodating a wide range of GT cars. The class was split into three categories—GTS-1, -2, and -3, which brought in a large and diverse group of newer FIA-approved cars and older IMSA cars. A total of thirty-three Porsche 911 Turbos and non-turbos started the race along with two BMW M-3s, two Callaway Corvettes, two Saleen Mustangs, a Lister Storm, a Dodge Viper, and a slew of tube-frame American Camaros, Oldsmobile Auroras, and Cutlass Supremes. Two Mazda RX-7s and an Acura NSX represented the Japanese brands.

The Porsche 911 GT2 of Roock Racing with Ralf Kelleners, Patrice Goueslard, Claudia Hürtgen, and André Ahrlé finished fourth overall to win the GTS-2 trophy. They were one position ahead of the GTS-1 class-winning Porsche Evo version called the 911 Turbo, entered by Jochen Rohr and co-driven with Andy Pilgrim, Harald Grohs, and Arnd Meier. Tom Milner's Prototype Technology Group BMW M3 driven by Bill Auberlen, Boris Said, Javier Quiros, and Derek Hill captured GTS-3, coming home in ninth overall.

This would be the last 24 Hours of Daytona sanctioned under the PSR or IMSA brand for many years. The sanctioning body had already ceased being the source of prize money paid to entrants. After the purse paying issues under Mike Cone, Daytona track officials had escrowed the purse and set up a specific account to have it appear that IMSA was processing the payments. In fact, the Speedway did the payout to the agreed upon schedule. Not until the 2000 race, when the IMSA-derived Grand American Road Racing Association, or Grand-Am, assumed control of the event, would it revert to the original process of the sanctioning body paying the purse money.

Round two, the 12 Hours of Sebring, became a controversial event under the PSR sanction. Where the turnout of cars at Daytona had been encouraging, officiating irregularities at Sebring began to severely undermine faith in Evans's leadership. Allegations abounded among competitors that PSR ownership was communicating instructions to race control from Pit Lane to manipulate full course yellows to give an advantage to the Scandia Ferrari.

When MOMO team manager Kevin Doran and team owner Moretti protested the officiating during the afternoon portion of the race while standing on Pit Lane, there was a reset in the scoring that included the Dyson Racing No. 16, which returned the cars of both teams to the lead lap. But during a battle for the lead in the late stages at night between Evans's Scandia Ferrari and the No. 16, the Ferrari gained almost an entire lap lead over the Dyson car due to confusion over the pace car procedures.

There was no official protest and Scandia cruised to the win in a race where fifteen WSC cars started. The second Doyle Racing Oldsmobile

A nighttime stop and driver change for the Doyle-Risi Ferrari. *Rick Dole*

Aurora R&S MK III, entered by Dibos Racing, scored its second consecutive third-place podium in two races with Pace, Peruvian Dibos, and Barry Waddell driving.

George Robinson, Jack Baldwin, and Hoerr captured GTS-1 in Robinson's Oldsmobile Aurora, which finished sixth overall. It beat the Porsche Turbo of Rohr, Pilgrim, and Robert Nearn by just over one minute. The Porsche GT2 owned by Franz Konrad and co-driven by Bob Wollek and Wido Roessler won the GTS-2 class, and PTG's BMW M3 was once again the GTS-3 winner in ninth overall, just as at Daytona.

Dyson Racing's No. 20 R&S-Ford finished fifth at Sebring, which kept Forbes-Robinson in the points lead for the Exxon World Sports Car Championship, an advantage due to pit choices always going to the team leading the points. The fate of the No. 20 was confirmed, and it would contest the balance of the season with Forbes-Robinson as the lead driver along with Paul Jr. in the quest for the championship. The lineup would be switched as

Synonymous with IMSA, the Porsches of Alex Job and Konrad Motorsport go door-to-door at Daytona. *Lee Self*

needed, always giving the Dyson team's drivers the best opportunity to maintain the points lead and to potentially win the title.

By season's end, Leitzinger earned the driving title following one victory with Weaver at Road Atlanta, one with Weaver and Forbes-Robinson at Watkins Glen, and two with Paul Jr., including the season finale at Laguna Seca. Forbes-Robinson finished second and Weaver third in the championship, giving Dyson a podium sweep.

The first sprint race of the season at Road Atlanta featured an eighteen-car WSC only grid. Dyson Racing dominated with a one-two finish ahead of the MOMO Ferrari, the car in which Andrea Montermini made his first IMSA start. The newcomer dazzled the series several times during the year with brilliantly quick driving. The MSI Chevrolet R&S MK III driven by Ross Bentley and Jeff Jones scored a strong fourth-place finish.

Following the Sebring controversy, the Scandia team withdrew from competition. For the balance of the year, the two Ferraris were entered either by the team of Eduardo Dibos or under the Central Arkansas Racing Services Banner of Charles and

Ron Fellows co-drove the Acxiom 333SP to victory at Mosport with Rob Morgan. The win on his home track in a Ferrari demonstrated the Canadian's versatility. *Rick Dole*

Rob Morgan. The Morgans first race in the Ferrari 333SP at Road Atlanta resulted in a fifth-place finish after co-driving the second Scandia car at Sebring.

Montermini broke through for wins with Antonio Hermann at Lime Rock, Pikes Peak, and the two-hour sprint race at Sebring, the next-to-last event. At Sears Point, having never been there before, he unofficially broke the WSC track record on only his third lap of the complex course! Rob Morgan and Canadian Ron Fellows took the Morgan team's lone Ferrari 333SP victory at Mosport, where regular Trans-Am and GT driver Fellows demonstrated his versatility on his home track in a rare appearance behind the wheel of a prototype.

GT remained a three-class structure with new

Powered by a front-mounted Ford V8, the Panoz Esperante GTR-1 won the GTS-1 class at Road Atlanta in the hands of Doc Bundy and Andy Wallace. *Rick Dole*

and interesting cars regularly arriving on the scene. In GTS-1, a pair of Don Panoz's front-engine Panoz GTR-1s—wheeled by Doc Bundy, Andy Wallace, David Brabham, and Eric Bernard—scored wins at Road Atlanta, Watkins Glen, Sears Point, and Laguna Seca. They were challenged all season by Andy Pilgrim and Allan McNish, co-drivers in Rohr's Porsche 911 Turbo. Pilgrim and McNish won four of the last five races to clinch the Exxon Supreme GTS-1 title for Pilgrim.

Nine of the GTS-1 races were won by the Panoz or Rohr's Porsche Turbo. Stu Hayner and Roger Schramm took a victory at Lime Rock in the Rock Valley Camaro, the only other IMSA tube-frame car victory after the Olds Aurora win at Sebring. The GTS-2 title went to Schumacher, who drove his team's atmospheric Porsche 911 RSR. PTG's Auberlen secured the GTS-3 championship.

The number of entries was consistently plentiful, enough that only Daytona, Sebring, and Watkins Glen ran a combined field of WSC cars and the three GT classes. The GT entrants ran eight separate races lasting a standard one hour and forty-five minutes.

Early in 1997, litigation was settled between PSR and the Sports Car Club of America over the use of the name Professional SportsCar Racing. It was just the beginning of constant issues under Evans's ownership. As the season progressed, the Evans-led IMSG group delivered no additional sponsorships or major new corporate partners. By mid-season, teams and drivers were becoming more and more concerned as posted prize money was not being paid and there was no visible progress on the marketing side. Gloom and doom were growing everywhere throughout the paddocks.

Canadian fans turned out in large numbers at Mosport for the long-standing IMSA race date. *Rick Dole*

The BMW M3s of Tom Milner and his Prototype Technology Group challenged the Porsche armada in the GTS-3 class. *Rick Dole*

The traditional Memorial Day race in Lime Rock once again proved popular with New England fans. *Rick Dole*

## RACKETS AND SCAMS

From Rob Dyson

"With Andy Evans, you always had a sense deep down inside that this guy was going to create trouble. Just the way he comported himself, especially in competition. He screwed us twice at Sebring.

"Tres Stevans, the Sebring general manager, was a witness to the fact that Evans was calling up race control during the twelve hour in 1997 to call for yellow flags that allowed his guys at Scandia to get in front of our car. When it was best for his team, he was saying, 'Put the yellow out.' Twice, his driver Yannick Dalmas got in front after he did this. We should have won the race, but the perversion of the yellow flag process purely to help Evans and his team was unprecedented. It was manipulated.

"Evans had a propensity to piss everybody off. That led me to conversations with Skip Barber, owner of Lime Rock and a well-respected figure in the industry. I said to Skip, 'This guy is just flat bad.' And then I called Bill France Jr. because I was on the International Speedway Corporation board then. I said, 'Bill, this guy is bad for business. We have got to stop this guy. He's wrecking sports car racing.'

"Among other things, Evans alleged that he had a copyright from Ferrari and other special industry relationships, which were probably not true and seemed to be conflicts of interest. He implied a special relationship with Bill Gates, which was murky. Evans was obviously a swindler.

"Later in the 1997 season, Evans called me up and said, 'Can I come to your office in New York?' He

After a long wait, Dyson celebrated a Rolex 24 victory in 1997. *Rick Dole*

Victory Lane at the Rolex 24 in 1997 included seven drivers (from left): James Weaver, John Schneider, Rob Dyson, Elliott Forbes-Robinson, and John Paul Jr. In front are Andy Wallace and Butch Leitzinger. *Rick Dole*

arrived about 5:30 one night. He said, 'I am going to do a RICO [Racketeer Influenced and Corrupt Organization Act] claim against Bill France, Roger Penske, Carl Haas, and the SCCA. These guys are damaging my reputation.' He then says, 'I'm looking for a buyer for IMSA.' I looked at him and said, 'Well, let me think about it.'

"Toward the end of 1997, Evans had not paid any prize money. To anybody . . . Nothing. He owed me a lot of money. There were millions and millions of unpaid bills. I thought about it for half an hour. I said to myself, 'I can't trust anything.'"

As a result of a trip to Japan with IMSA, Butch Leitzinger began spelling his name in Japanese katakana script on the side of his helmet. *Rick Dole*

Ross Bentley and Jeff Jones shared a Riley & Scott MK III-Chevrolet. *Rick Dole*

## EVANS ABDICATES

The season ended with Evans abdicating ownership of IMSA/PSR by giving it to a group of four individuals. In October, this group signed a letter of intent —via a company called PSR Holdings—to acquire the sanctioning body. Eventually, Evans handed them the rights to the IMSA name, the company's stock in 25 percent portions, and a hefty amount of debt and unpaid bills.

The new ownership group consisted of Mike Gue, Ray Smith, Doug Robinson, and Tom Milner. Gue, owner of Essex Racing and an IMSA entrant throughout the 1980s and 1990s, became president and took control of the day-to-day operation. He was the logical choice to lead the group, being well respected in the paddock as a levelheaded business professional, a successful team owner, and a conduit for racing hardware from the UK. Smith, one of the financial advisors for Evans, took on the challenge of making the company financially whole again, having realized in his short tenure that the company had a good product and an impeccable history worth the massive effort of trying to save it.

Robinson, an ex-General Motors motorsport executive, transitioned from his role as a technical and rules administrator under Evans to become one of the principals of PSR Holdings. Milner, who had participated in IMSA since the 1970s, was an active team owner in the series at the time with his BMW M3 cars. He remained in the background to avoid conflicts of interest on the competition side.

In December, Gue and Smith entered acquisition negotiations with the Interpublic Group's

## TAKING OVER FROM EVANS

From Mike Gue

Michael Gue, a respected member of the IMSA community, fielded prototypes under his own Essex Racing banner. In addition, the Essex Racing parts business was a reliable source of components for racers. The winner of the 1988 Camel Lights team championship, Gue proved to be insightful during any discussions about the conduct of the series, and his viewpoint was appreciated by IMSA officials. After moving into the World Sports Car ranks, at the end of the 1996 season he elected to shut down the Essex Racing team while continuing in the parts business. He soon embarked on a very different journey.

"When the prize money started not being paid by Andy Evans during the 1997 season, I got really annoyed. Tom Milner, a fellow team principal and another long-standing member of the original IMSA community, started talking to me. He said, 'Well, you should do something about it.' He encouraged me to get involved with brokering a deal between Evans and Octagon, which had expressed an interest in acquiring PSR/IMSA from Evans.

"Andy liked the idea of Octagon being interested in taking over PSR, so in conjunction with Ray Smith, Andy's financial consultant, and Doug Robinson, PSR's technical manager, we started negotiations. I ended up brokering this because of having a relationship of sorts with Andy when I was fielding Kudzu Camel Light cars. Andy wanted out and did not want to see PSR/IMSA go under and disappear during his ownership.

"We crafted a plan that we felt was a good starting point. At first, Andy wanted me to get all the teams together and suggested PSR could operate like a franchise system. I said, 'That's fine, except you have zero credibility with anybody. Nobody wants to do business with you.' At that time, Ray and some team owners were sitting in on the phone conversations. I insisted that they could listen but could not participate, as I did not want the conversation to turn into a free-for-all.

"We got it to a point where Andy said, 'I want somebody to take it on, and I'm prepared to let it go.'

"Les Delano, who had participated in a handful of IMSA GT races in the 1980s and 1990s, was the contact at Octagon. He asked me to start discussions with Smith, Robinson, and Milner. Delano made it clear that as a public company Octagon could not be seen to be negotiating with anyone. If we could take over ownership of PSR/IMSA, he told us, and establish a timeline to clean it up, Octagon could come back to purchase it without all the warts and blemishes.

"Octagon took an option to purchase PSR/IMSA from the four of us after we had acquired it and cleaned up the books.

"We set up the holding company to acquire the PSR/IMSA stock from Andy under the name of PSR Holdings. By December, we negotiated an agreement and planned to make an announcement at the Performance Racing Industry show. The four of us agreed that if we had not got his signature on the agreement, the deal was off. When the announcement meeting started, we still had not got Andy's signature. When I got up to speak, I had two scripts. One said it was all over and the other that we had a deal. At the last minute, Ray called and said the deal was on."

newly formed sports marketing agency Octagon, which was led in the US by occasional IMSA racers Les Delano and Andy Petery. An option for Octagon to purchase PSR/IMSA was agreed upon and a deposit made. Earlier in the 1990s, Delano and Petery had been heavily involved in negotiations with IMSA's Silbermann and Raffauf as a potential buyer of IMSA from Cone. Slater ended up with that deal, but Delano and Petery, advertising executives of note, always remained on friendly terms.

Because of the ongoing controversies during the 1997 season, the unpaid prize money, and the need for road racing events at its tracks, the International Speedway Corporation (ISC) began heading in a new direction for 1998. ISC elected to drop Professional SportsCar Racing and instead joined forces with the SCCA to sanction and operate sports car races under a new series banner.

It decided to revive the United States Road Racing Championship (USRRC) from the 1960s as the name of the new series set to begin in 1998. For the first time since 1975, IMSA would not sanction the famed twenty-four-hour endurance race that opened the world's circuit racing calendar every January at Daytona International Speedway. A sports car racing divergence in the US was beginning, one that would continue for almost two decades. Two different philosophies and business models for sports car racing would vie for success in the same market.

The schedule for the first season of the new USRRC included the Rolex 24 Hours at Daytona, the Watkins Glen Six Hour, and a sprint race at Homestead Miami Speedway—all ISC tracks. A street race in Minneapolis that was already on the existing SCCA Trans-Am calendar and the independent Mid-Ohio Sports Car Course completed the proposed five-race schedule for 1998.

The France family, which controlled the tracks owned by ISC, focused on self-reliance and sustainability for their businesses. These were the key elements that brought Bill France Jr. and Jim France, the sons of NASCAR founder "Big Bill" France, continued success after assuming command of the family business. The brothers went into expansion mode in 1996 after a public offering of ISC stock, which later included a merger of ISC and the circuits owned by Roger Penske. Penske operated his tracks on a similar philosophy, and the merger confirmed the Frances' business model was built for long term success.

In addition to track ownership, the Frances fully owned NASCAR, which was booming and experiencing huge gains on all fronts. On the sports car side, the ISC principals, including Bill France Jr.'s daughter Lesa France Kennedy, were concerned with issues in Europe as well as what was viewed as the instability of PSR.

They had watched the FIA and Le Mans path diverge from a potentially sustainable and practical Group C prototype series in the early 1990s to a failed 3.5-liter prototype option of greater cost. This was followed by a GT-1-based top class for only a few years and then a swing back to boosting prototypes with an LMP-1 category that was based on the IMSA WSC class.

A European-based series and set of rules controlled by Le Mans and its ACO organizers did not coincide with the business model in Daytona. The constant altering required a lot of very expensive equipment to be bought (if available) or heavily changed to compete with factories for a win. The rules obsoleted a lot of perfectly good hardware that was working well in the US. At one point it was overheard in Daytona that "the Atlantic Ocean isn't big enough," a reference to the vast gap between how the Frances approached racing and the European method.

The lack of faith in Evans's leadership and occasional statements about adopting the same approach for PSR as used in Europe reinforced the decision by the principals in Daytona to embark in a new direction.

EXXON
Valvoline
EXXON
YOKOHAMA
BMW Financial Services
Hella
Hella
BMW CCA
YOKOHAMA
harman/kardon
EXXON
Red Bull
FINA
FINA
Hella
harman/kardon
41
EXXON
EXXON
EXXON
EXXON
EXXON

## CHAPTER NINE

# 1998: THE SPLIT BEGINS

The revived United States Road Racing Championship season opener drew a strong seventy-four-car entry to the Rolex 24 at Daytona to launch the sports car competition in 1998. Many entries came from teams that had contested the race the year before, drawn back by the challenge of the twenty-four-hour race on Daytona's high banks as well as by the prospect of a new series under the sanction of the SCCA.

The structure of the rules remained similar, but the World Sports Car class was renamed Can-Am, another term revived from one of the sanctioning body's past series: the Canadian American Challenge Cup. In the absence of the brand sponsorship from Exxon Supreme, the *S* was dropped from the GT class names.

Though it was not an IMSA-sanctioned race, key players from the PSR/IMSA ranks still participated in it. The result was one of the most popular wins in American sports car racing history. Gentleman racer Gianpiero Moretti, a longtime IMSA supporter who had spent twenty years trying to capture the Rolex 24, won in his MOMO-branded Ferrari 333SP that was fielded by Doran Racing Enterprises. His co-drivers Arie Luyendyk, Mauro Baldi, and Didier Theys also won the coveted special edition Rolex Daytona watches. A well-circulated postrace photo showed the three co-drivers looking at the watch on Moretti's wrist after he unceremoniously opened the box and put his on in Victory Lane. Not incidentally, this was the first time Ferrari won a twenty-four-hour race since Daytona in 1967.

The victory culminated a long love affair between Moretti and the Daytona twenty-four hour, which started with his first race in 1970 on board a Ferrari 512. After some years away from racing, he resumed in 1979. He came oh so close several times at Daytona before late-race heartaches. In 1992, he was leading Sunday morning in

GT category action was close among many brands, but there were always a lot of Porsches. *Rick Dole*

a Joest 962 Porsche when the engine blew up. In 1993, the team was again leading with its Nissan NPT 90-91. Moretti had a large lead with less than two hours to go, but the engine failed again. Two years later, the 333SP, which Moretti had encouraged Ferrari to build, ran for the first time at Daytona, but all the V12 engines failed due to issues with sand and the valve seats.

Moretti's team had the famous battle with Wayne Taylor's Riley & Scott in 1996 only to lose in the closing minutes. Early in the race, Moretti, Theys, Papis, and Bob Wollek ran strongly enough to win. But two mufflers fell apart and had to be changed. They were leading Sunday when Wollek had a run-in with a GT car in the chicane, which caused damage and a long stay in the pits. Papis then drove the last hours and earned his nickname "Mad Max," making up the two lost laps only to fall sixty-two seconds short. The MOMO entry was again quick enough to win the following year, but a failure of a five dollar oil fitting caused a fire in the engine bay that burned up the wiring.

Two decades after his inaugural entry, Gianpiero Moretti co-drove to his first endurance victory at Daytona and claimed his Rolex watch. *Brian Cleary*

The Porsche contingent went door-to-door for class honors in GTS-1 against Panoz Racing throughout the season.
*Rick Dole*

It seemed only fair that Moretti finally got his Rolex after two decades of trying.

The GT1 category was well subscribed with eighteen entries and led by cars designed for competition at Le Mans under ACO rules. The USRRC gave these entries weight penalties to help pave the way for a Can-Am class victory and keep prototypes as the premier category. The question of whether GT cars should be able to race for the overall victory was at the heart of the debate over the future of sports car racing.

Determined to try to win overall with their GT cars, both the Panoz GTR-1 and Porsche 911 GT1 entries were highly competitive despite additional weight. But no entries were as fast as the Dyson team's Riley & Scott MK III prototype. The Panoz GTR-1 dropped out with a blown engine just before dawn, soon followed to the sidelines by the Dyson team due to engine problems. That left the door open for the MOMO Ferrari—and an opportunity to repair a suspension problem on Pit Road without losing the lead.

The Porsche GT1 entries had not been as fast as the Panoz, but after the departure of the GTR-1, the Rohr Motorsports team came on to claim the class victory and second overall with drivers Allan McNish, Uwe Alzen, Dirk Müller, Jörg Müller, and Danny Sullivan. Konrad Motorsport's Porsche GT2 and Prototype Technology Group's BMW M3 claimed the GT2 and GT3 victories.

Politics played out in reverse fashion at the second major race of the sports car season when PSR/IMSA hosted the 12 Hours of Sebring. The controversy at Sebring the year before and the ongoing issue of unpaid purses were both still hanging in the air along with the more traditional aroma of orange blossoms. Only forty-eight entries started the classic twelve-hour enduro—which was

Wayne Taylor returned to a Ferrari 333SP in 1998, partnering his own Doyle-backed team with Giuseppe Risi's Houston-based crew. *Rick Dole*

Butch Leitzinger won back-to-back championships at Dyson Racing in the team's potent R&S MK III-Ford.
*Rick Dole*

the first event for the newly formed PSR Holdings group that took over from Andy Evans—compared with the seventy-four starters at Daytona.

Panoz Racing had debuted the dramatically swoopy GTR-1, sometimes known as the Batmobile, at the previous year's Sebring race. The Ford-powered, front-engine car was designed and built by Adrian Reynard. He first met Don Panoz while visiting the specialty street car manufacturing operation of his son, Danny Panoz, who had a small factory near Road Atlanta. Reynard suggested that with the right car Don Panoz could win the 24 Hours of Le Mans. Panoz asked Reynard to build a front-engine GT racer because that was the configuration of his son's upcoming Esperante sports cars. Thus, an iconic racing vehicle was born, one that launched Panoz's fascination with Le Mans, which in turn led to a significant role for him in the future of IMSA.

Having purchased Road Atlanta in 1996, Panoz was already active as a track owner. One year after making his team's racing debut at Sebring, He returned as the owner of the lease on the Florida track and would soon add the Mosport Park circuit in Canada to his portfolio. By purchasing the latter two tracks from Evans, Panoz facilitated the departure of Evans from sports car racing.

Although the Panoz GTR-1 was competitive at Sebring, especially without the weight penalty at Daytona, it was Moretti's MOMO squad that captured the Sebring victory, becoming the fourth team to have won the 36 Hours of Florida back-to-back with the same car and drivers. The Panoz driven by David Brabham and Wallace finished second overall, a lap down and first in GT1. Porsche captured GT2 with the 911 driven by Nick Ham and Franz Konrad. The Milner team's BMW M3 of Bill Auberlen, Boris Said, and Mark Simo won in GT3.

USRRC ran four more races after Daytona, averaging twenty-five entries per race. Dyson Racing won at Homestead and Minneapolis with Weaver and Leitzinger driving the team's R&S MK III-Ford and at Mid-Ohio, where its MK III was wheeled by Forbes-Robinson and Schroeder. Moretti, supported by co-drivers Baldi and Theys, won again in the six-hour race at Watkins Glen, becoming the first team to score a hat trick for all three major endurance races in North America in one season. The margin of victory was a narrow 0.656 seconds over the Dyson Racing MK III of Weaver, Leitzinger, and Forbes-Robinson.

In GT, Panoz Racing won at Homestead (Wallace/Bundy), Mid-Ohio (Eric Bernard/Raul Boesel), and in the streets of Minneapolis (Bundy/O'Connell) before finally being beaten by the Champion Porsche 911 GT1 Evo at Watkins Glen driven by Boutsen and Kelleners. A selection of

The Ferrari driven by Didier Theys demonstrates the classic 333SP "burn" of unspent fuel that came through the V12 engine. *Brian Cleary*

BMWs and Porsches shared GT2 and GT3 wins over the course of the short schedule. GT2 had low car counts and often teams moved their GT3 cars up, trying to nab a win in the under-supported class. The relatively short season concluded after the Watkins Glen event in August.

PSR/IMSA pushed ahead to complete its eight-race calendar with events at Las Vegas Motor Speedway, a Road Atlanta sprint race, and a round at Lime Rock—including the only solo GT race of the year. The series returned to Mosport, then ran a three-hour race at Sebring before heading back to Road Atlanta for the first 1,000-mile Petit Le Mans, and then concluded the season at Laguna Seca. The series also averaged twenty-five starters per event over the balance of the season.

Taylor had merged Doyle Racing with the famed Houston-based team of Risi Competizione—

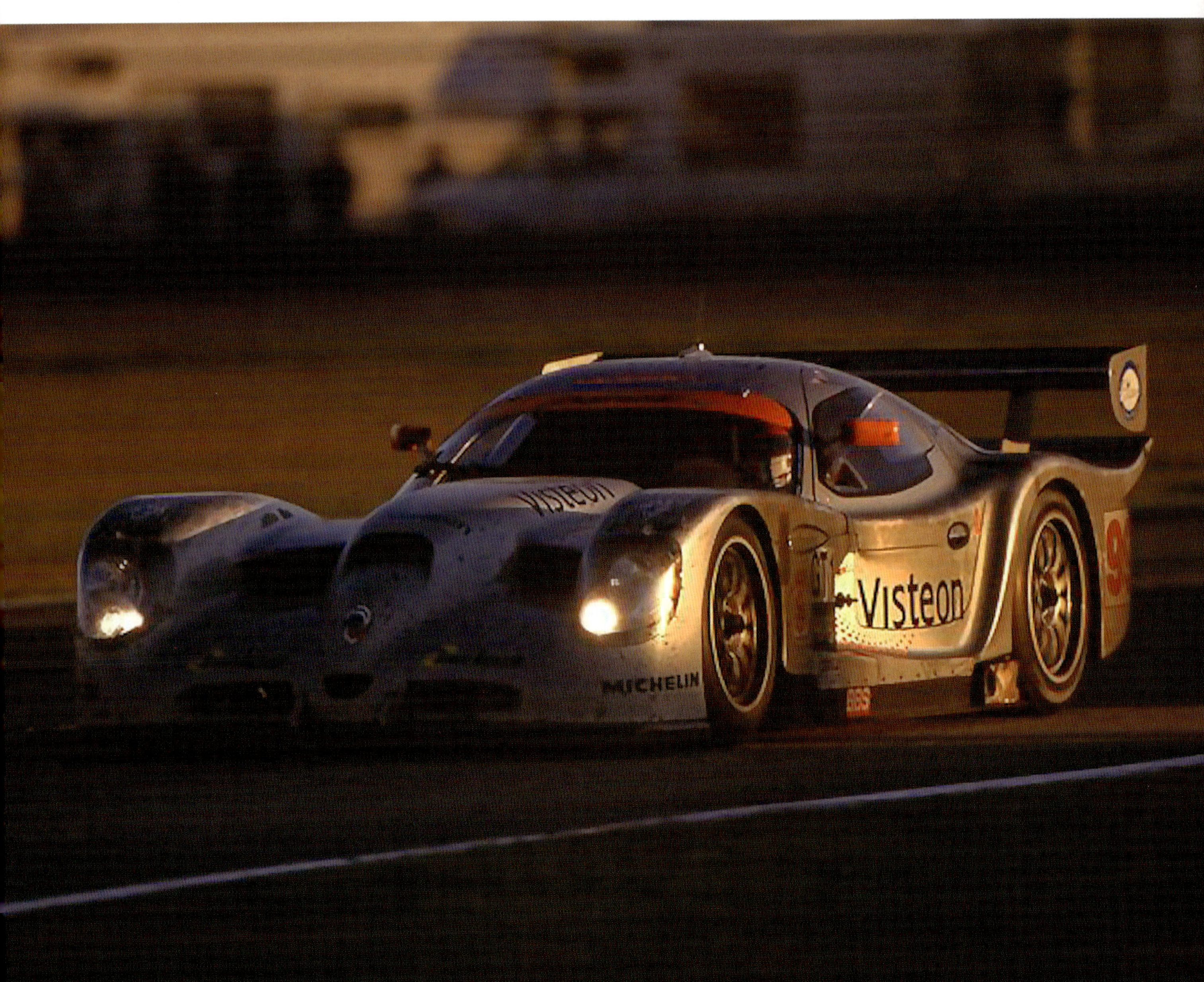


Drivers David Brabham and Andy Wallace scored five GTS-1 victories in the Panoz Esperante GTR-1. *Rick Dole*

Doyle-Risi Racing won the inaugural Petit Le Mans race at Road Atlanta. *Rick Dole*

owned by Giuseppe Risi—to create Doyle-Risi Racing, which campaigned a Ferrari 333SP with Taylor and van de Poele as the primary drivers. They won at Las Vegas and at the inaugural Petit Le Mans, adding Emmanuel Collard as the third driver. Dyson's Weaver and Leitzinger won at Lime Rock, Road Atlanta, and Mosport.

Brabham and Wallace finally scored an overall victory at the three-hour Sebring event in their Panoz GTR-1, which showed how potent the FIA GT1 category cars were becoming, especially in the rain when heavier cars gain an advantage due to more weight on the tires and better grip. Weaver and Leitzinger were second overall and first in WSC once again.

During the season, Gue and Smith of PSR Holdings earned credibility with their efforts behind the scenes. They paid off the purses from the previous year, maintained operations, and enforced regulations.

The pitched battle between the Panoz Racing entries and the Porsches featured unique cars and world class drivers. *Rick Dole*

Some of the funding to pay overdue purses came from an option-to-buy contract made between PSR Holdings and Octagon. A marketing company already involved in racing, Octagon had been negotiating to buy IMSA. Octagon forfeited its option-to-buy payment after negotiations floundered and no purchase was made by the agreed upon date.

Additional funding came from Exxon, which had withheld some cash support in 1997 during its final year of title sponsorship due to concerns with the management of the Evans group. That money was instead given to PSR Holdings in 1998, with the understanding that it would be used by Gue and Smith to help pay down the previous season's outstanding purse obligations to teams.

Midway through 1998, negotiations were reopened with the Interpublic-owned Octagon agency, which made a second payment for the right of first refusal on any sale of PSR Holdings. Due to complications and the unsustainability of the planned business model proposed by Octagon, once again a deal was not completed. A new option in the form of Don Panoz began to emerge.

## THE MOMO MAN GETS HIS ROLEX

By Martin Raffauf

Gianpiero Moretti competed in his first Rolex 24 at Daytona in 1970 on board a Ferrari 512 S entered by Squadra Picchio-Rosso that failed to finish. Eight years later, he became an IMSA regular and began his annual quest to win at Daytona, an effort that finally became successful in 1998 on board his Ferrari 333SP.

In the early years, he drove Porsches 935s followed by a variety of GTP cars, starting with an Alba AR5, March82G-Buick, and Ford Mustang Probe. He then took up the cudgel with Porsche 962s, a Spice SE89P, and a Nissan NPT-90 before striking gold—as in a Rolex watch—with the Ferrari 333SP.

By the 1990s, Moretti had the most career starts in IMSA's top classes. A fan favorite, he frequently invited competitors and fans to a pasta feast at the track with his team. Sponsored by his MOMO company, which manufactured steering wheels and car accessories,

Intent on getting his first Rolex 24 winner's watch, Gianpiero Moretti kept his head and foot down onboard his Ferrari.
*Brian Cleary*

The high-revving, sixty-valve iron block V12 was the power plant used in Ferrari's F50 road car. *Bill Tuttle*

Moretti's racing activities around the world helped make it a well-known automotive brand.

Gianpiero had a love affair with the Daytona twenty-four hour. He wanted to win it at least once before he retired, and he came close to winning several times before succeeding. In 1992, he was leading Sunday morning in a Joest Porsche 962 when the engine blew up. In 1993, his team was leading again in a Nissan NPT-90 with under two hours remaining when the engine expired.

Recognizing the opportunity presented by the Ferrari brand and its potential at Daytona, Moretti helped IMSA representatives persuade Piero Ferrari to build the 333SP, which ran for the first time at Daytona in 1995. That year the Ferrari engines all failed due to valve seat issues. The seats were wearing away due to bad materials, and a poor air filter design allowed the Daytona sand to get into the engine, which did not help matters. Ferrari officials had told the teams the engines would not last twenty-four hours. It turned out they were correct.

In 1996, the MOMO Corse team had the famous battle with the Riley & Scott MK III-Olds of Doyle Racing and Wayne Taylor. Moretti co-drove with Didier Theys, Max Papis, and Bob Wollek. Two mufflers fell apart and had to be changed. Yet, they still had a chance to win and were leading Sunday when Wollek suffered contact from an errant GT car in the chicane, which caused damage that resulted in a long pit stop. Max Papis then drove the final hours, earning his nickname "Mad Max." He made up two lost laps but fell sixty-two seconds short at the end. In 1997, the car was again quick enough to win, but the failure of a five dollar oil fitting caused a fire in the engine bay, which burned up the wiring.

By 1998, teams had figured out how to sustain the 333SP for twenty-four hours, which came down to preparation and execution. Kevin Doran, the owner of Doran Racing Enterprises, prepared Moretti's cars and had won the Daytona twenty-four hour twice in the 1980s as the team manager for Al Holbert and Holbert Racing. Most of the crew on the MOMO entry, led by chief mechanic Jeff Graves, had been with Kevin since the Ferrari 333SP first came to IMSA in 1994.

For 1998, the team had a great driver lineup with Moretti, Didier Theys, and Mauro Baldi, who had been drivers of the 333SP since its arrival. They were joined by Arie Luyendyk, who was Theys's neighbor in Scottsdale, Arizona. Luyendyk had won the Indianapolis 500 twice, Sebring once, and had driven Nissan prototypes in endurance events. He fit in like he had been on the team for years.

For the second straight year, the race would be hotly contested between the R&S MK III-Fords and the Ferraris. Of the six Fords, the strongest were the brace of MK IIIs of Dyson Racing. The Ferrari protagonists were Doran/Moretti Racing, Doyle-Risi

Rob Dyson was among the many congratulating Moretti as he headed down Pit Road to Victory Lane. *Brian Cleary*

Breaking tradition, Gianpiero put on his Rolex in Victory Lane. *Rick Dole*

Racing, and a Scandia Motorsport entry from Andy Evans.

The Ferrari was well suited to Daytona, which favored top speed. It was powered by a 4.0-liter V12 and had a slight edge in horsepower over the Ford V8 but had a disadvantage when it came to torque.

With some superstition, Doran took the pit location adjacent to the break in the wall on Pit Road, where a winning car would turn left to get into Victory Lane after a race. Moretti started the race, but in the first stint had an altercation with a GT car that caused some damage to the bodywork on the right rear and the right-rear wing plate. It was repaired with tape over the next several pit stops, and the car continued.

When IMSA officials complained about no right-side number, which had been taken off in the incident, the team fashioned its No. 30 out of yellow tape and put it on the wing end plate during one of the subsequent pit stops. The car looked a little second-hand, but it continued with good pace.

The MOMO team celebrating at Daytona. Finally! *Rick Dole*

During the night, the team got lucky. Luyendyk had a tire fail coming into the Daytona tri-oval at over 190 miles per hour. Maybe his Indy car experience helped him as he spun to his left and missed the wall, ending up in Pit Lane, very near the team's pit stall. The huge spin resulted in a quick chassis check and a change of tires before the car was sent on its way!

By Sunday morning the Doran/Moretti Ferrari was back to second place. One of the two Dyson cars was leading, and the second had been retired. The two other Ferrari competitors were also out. The Doyle-Risi car had crashed in the early evening and the Evans car had terminal issues in the engine and gearbox.

Everyone knew from the previous year that the Dyson Fords were straining to finish twenty-four hours. Although they won in 1997, the car had struggled at the end.

Sunday morning, Doran elected to start pushing the pace harder, making the Dyson team run faster to stay ahead. The Dyson car started smoking and running five seconds a lap slower. A short while later, the car came into the pits in a big cloud of smoke and steam. The engine had expired. The Daytona twenty-four hour brought out as much emotion in team owner Rob Dyson as it did in Moretti. After he completed the painful TV interviews about his team's failed effort, Dyson, a true sportsman, came down to the MOMO squad's pit box and hung out almost until the end of the race.

At the finish, following a long stop for precautionary suspension repairs, Moretti took the checkered flag. All the teams lined Pit Lane in salute and applauded as he rolled down Pit Road. A Ferrari had won the 24 Hours of Daytona for the first time since 1967. The church bells were ringing in Maranello. It was front page news in Italy.

Victory Lane was surreal. As they handed out the Rolex watches, Moretti started to open the packaging and take his watch out. This was not done before. Most drivers just smiled and accepted the Rolex box. Someone asked, "What are you doing Gianpiero?" He said, "I have spent hundreds of thousands of dollars to get this watch. I am going to put it on now!"

The co-drivers join their team owner in trying on their new watches. *Rick Dole*

## CASH CONUNDRUMS AND THE SUPERBIKE MODEL

From Mike Gue

"Going into the 1998 season, we were struggling, because everybody was completely disenchanted by Andy Evans from the antics of the previous season. Our number one goal was to reestablish the credibility of PSR/IMSA and be incorruptible in operating a race rule book, for both the little guy and in the eyes of the major manufacturers.

"I asked Ray Smith to provide a financial cash flow estimate, what money we were going to need over the year from an operating point of view and what assets we had. I wanted to know what sources for money we thought were available to us through unpaid sponsorship, Octagon commitments, and other possible sources of money.

"Our biggest challenge was making good in some way for the unpaid prize money from 1997. We gave teams two options. First, we communicated with them that if you stick with PSR through May with race entries, we should be able to pay 50 percent of what you were owed from the previous year. The second choice was sticking with PSR to the end of the year. We committed to pay 70 percent of what was owed, but again, no guarantee.

"Every team, except one, accepted the 70 percent offer. I took that as a huge vote of confidence, but it put an additional strain on the budget, as I had convinced Ray that no one would take the 70 percent deal!

"So, we were considering how to come up with the prize money we committed to from 1997 along with the necessary operating budget to complete the year.

"By May, we had enough money because we found out by chance that Exxon had withheld certain fees payable from 1997. Ray contacted the financial people at Exxon and got a very nice reception. He was told the money had already been accounted for but was held back because they wanted to see what happened with Andy. They didn't understand the details of what we were doing but recognized things were going forward and wired us the money.

"It was a six-figure sum. With this money and what we had received from Octagon, which was a substantial six-figure option, we were able to meet the May deadline and pay the teams.

"Octagon had bought the World Super Bike Series and they wanted us to see if the sanctioning model they used for the Super Bike Series could be used for our series. The model being used in that series that was proposed by Les Delano and Octagon to also be used for IMSA was not practical. They expected to ask tracks for a large sanctioning fee and complete control of the paddock.

"Using [the] Super Bike model, IMSA would get a fee and control all the commercial interests of the event. The circuits, according to Octagon, were supposed to make their money on sales of tickets, food, and souvenirs, plus a portion of the advertising revenue. We never got as far as who would control the rights to TV. Eventually, it all came down to me saying to Les, 'There's no circuit in this country that is going to pay anything close to your expected sanction fee for an event. There is no circuit in this country that is going to give us complete control and access to the paddock.' As a result of this impasse, the option period ran out. They continued to show interest and there was talk about them joining forces with Panoz, but that never progressed.

"We saw our jobs to be sustaining the future of PSR/IMSA, and at that point Panoz stepped in, and we signed up to sanction the ALMS series for the 1999 season."

## THE FIRST PETIT LE MANS

From Mike Gue

"The first Petit Le Mans event was contracted as part of an existing PSR scheduled date at Road Atlanta in the fall. The negotiations with the Automobile Club de l'Ouest and Don were frosty at times as they wanted complete control of the event without accepting any of the liability, and they wanted all the pomp and circumstance that exists at the Le Mans event.

"Don said he wanted to have scrutineering at Lenox Square near downtown Atlanta. I said 'Really? A shopping mall as a background compared with the cathedral in Le Mans? Really?' So, he arranged it all. I confirmed I would have a whole tech crew and do tech there at the shopping center with the public invited as they do in Le Mans. All this did was upset most of the patrons of Lenox Square, because there was nowhere to park. But car guys were interested and wandered around.

"Who was going to run the race was another major hurdle to overcome. We had a contract with the American Le Mans Series to run the event, but rules and regulations were a constant ongoing discussion with the ACO and Don. The rights to conduct the race were held by PSR, because it was a member of Automobile Competition Committee of the US, which was recognized by the FIA. Despite their desire to run the race, neither a foreign organization like the ACO nor the ALMS were functioning entities in the US at that time when it came to conducting races.

"FIA president Max Mosley reaffirmed PSR/IMSA to be the organization that had listed the race

Parallel to establishing a successful reputation in the US, at Le Mans, and in the FIA GT series as a team owner, Panoz began looking into becoming a series operator. His first step was establishing a contract agreement with the ACO that allowed him to brand a series in the US with the Le Mans name and to use the Le Mans rule book. In January 1998, he announced the first Petit Le Mans at Road Atlanta, and in June at Le Mans he announced the formation of the American Le Mans Series for the following season.

Leading up to the inaugural running of the 1,000-mile Petit, Panoz and the ACO had every intention of taking control and managing the event themselves. But IMSA, although not a name publicly used by PSR, continued to be recognized as the board member of the Automobile Competition Committee of the United States (ACCUS). ACCUS, in turn, was the national sporting authority recognized by the FIA, which controlled the listings for events on the international calendar, a critical element in licensing, driver participation, and insurance.

There was a lot of discussion about using the same rules as Le Mans prior to the first Petit and whether Panoz should run the event along with ACO officials. It was pointed out that Panoz and the ACO had no insurance and would not be able to purchase it on short notice without control of the sanctioning body. Following confirmation from FIA President Max Mosley that PSR/IMSA retained control due to its listing on the FIA International event calendar, Panoz and the ACO officials at Road Atlanta grudgingly acknowledged the event would be run by Gue and his staff once the sanctioning fee was paid. With few exceptions, the race's operational rules conformed to those used by PSR all season.

A large crowd showed up to watch twenty-nine starters, boosted by the support given to the race from Porsche, which brought its Le Mans–winning Porsche GT1-98 and funded the entry of Reinhold Joest's two-time Le Mans–winning LMP1 car. Porsche also took out billboards around the city of Atlanta that promoted the event and featured the GT1-98. The race's most dramatic moment took place when the vaunted GT1-98, in the hands of

on the FIA's international calendar and made it clear PSR, as the group who had submitted the listing, had to be the entity operating it. This along with the late realization by both Panoz and the ACO that they had none of the required liability insurance or medical accident insurance in the US, and were unlikely to achieve it, slowly pushed everyone to the realization that PSR should and would run the event in its entirety. Beyond the issue of insurance and event liability, PSR had the people in place.

"There ended up being multiple classes at the first Petit. A combination of ACO and PSR classes gave just about everyone a class. ACO did not like pace cars or the way PSR used wave arounds under cautions. They did not like refueling and making tire changes at the same time. There was only so much we could change from our regular season rules. But we had to change something, so we adopted an ACO rule that if you stopped on the circuit, you were out of the race. This approach was never a part of IMSA or PSR's original philosophy, but it initially worked at placating the ACO.

"Literally the night before the start of the race, the ACO and Panoz were still pushing me for the ACO's officials to run the race and suggested PSR's race director Marty Kaufmann could stand behind them and advise them. We would not allow this to happen. Eventually, I had to ask all the same questions again. 'Where's your insurance? Who accepts the liability?' Finally, the ACO acquiesced, and we were in charge and the ACO officials were invited into Race Control to observe.

"The race had an excellent fan turnout and was a huge success."

Yannick Dalmas, did a backflip coming over the rise after Turn Eight. Fortunately, the car spun 360 degrees and landed on its back wheels before angling off into the guardrail.

The winning Doyle-Risi Ferrari finished a little more than a minute ahead of the Joest Porsche LMP1, the same car withdrawn from Daytona a few years earlier over a regulation disagreement. The start featured a mix of IMSA-classed cars in the WSC and GT ranks and twelve ACO-classed cars (LMP1, LM GT1, and LM GT2). The ACO class winners received automatic entry invitations to the following year's 24 Hours of Le Mans if they chose to race the same car. For several European-based teams, that was a strong incentive to travel to Georgia to contest the race.

The final event of the season, which reverted to PSR/IMSA classes, found a young star emerging from Laguna Seca after a rare race in the rain at the "Dry Lake." Driving with extraordinary verve on a rapidly drying track in an entry started by Didier de Radiguès, Bill Auberlen came from thirty-two seconds behind in just fourteen laps to win overall in the Team Rafanelli BMW-powered Riley & Scott MK III. A regular winner in GT cars, it was Auberlen's first prototype victory.

Leitzinger, who had a breakout season the previous year, took a second WSC Championship from Taylor by finishing fourth overall and second in the WSC class with co-driver Weaver.

Brabham outdueled fellow Panoz driver Bernard in the mixed conditions during the closing minutes to claim the GT1 title with co-driver Wallace. Schumacher co-drove a steady race in his Porsche to clinch the GT2 title with a fourth-place finish. Auberlen, who had started the race in PTG's No. 1 BMW, narrowly lost the GT3 title when a WSC entry crashed and collected Peter Cunningham, his co-driver. Mark Simo came out as the class champion after finishing second in the No. 6 M3 that was started by Cunningham—a very busy driver on this day!

At season's end, Panoz opened negotiations with Gue and PSR Holdings to operate the inaugural American Le Mans Series season under contract in 1999.

GOOD YEAR
97 98
CHAMPIONS
GOODYEAR
#1 in Racing
Hella
PAGID
brake linings
BOSCH
USRRC
SHOEI

CHAPTER TEN

# 1999: THE SPLIT CONTINUES

The inaugural season of the American Le Mans Series in 1999 brought new manufacturer and team involvement in addition to the privateer regulars fielding World Sports Cars. The series was conducted under a contract between owner Panoz and PSR Holdings, led by Gue.

The new manufacturers resulted from the shift in focus to the categories of cars run at Le Mans under the ACO's sporting regulations—a founding principle of the ALMS. This included BMW's beautiful new V12 LMR prototype, which became a major player over the course of the season.

The Rolex 24 at Daytona opened the sports car racing calendar as was traditional, but it would become an abbreviated three-race season in just the second year of the US Road Racing Championship (USRRC). An impressive starting field of seventy-eight cars competed under USRRC rules for Can-Am prototypes, GT2, GT3, and GTT—the class for tube-frame American cars. Once again, Dyson Racing put its stout R&S MK III-Ford into Victory Lane, this time with the traditional count of three drivers—Forbes-Robinson, Leitzinger, and Wallace. The trio's R&S MK III was pursued over the long day and night grind by four Ferraris, but it outlasted them all.

USSRC would fade away to be replaced by something entirely different for 2000. The original schedule called for five events, but only three took place at Daytona, Lime Rock, and Mid-Ohio.

Theys and Lienhard won at Lime Rock in the Doran Racing Enterprises–prepared Lista Ferrari. Only twenty-four cars started in the combined Can-Am, GT2, and GT3 classes. The Ford versus Ferrari battles, which had continued uninterrupted since their first WSC competition in 1995, were coming to an end. At Mid-Ohio there were only twenty-one starters, with Dyson Racing's R&S MK III-Fords taking first and second. For the first time in four seasons, there were no Ferraris in the chase. The Mid-Ohio event closed

Dyson Racing won the Rolex 24 and the accompanying watches for a second time in three years. *Rick Dole*

the door on the USRRC, soon to be replaced by a new organization launched in Daytona Beach.

Embarking on an ambitious calendar, the ALMS season began at Sebring's twelve hour in March and included a spring event at Road Atlanta in addition to the Petit Le Mans, already established as a major endurance race after the large turnout of fans and participants in its first running. The race at Mosport was the fourth on the schedule at a track owned by series founder Panoz. The additional races at Sears Point, Portland, Laguna Seca, and Las Vegas were conducted as independently promoted events or as track rentals.

In addition to BMW's V12 LMR, also arriving for the first time at Sebring were the new twin-turbo Audi R8R, the Panoz LMP-1 Roadster S (introduced in April of the previous year), a Judd-powered R&S MK III, and several Lola B98/10s with Ford, BMW, and Lotus powerplants. The BMW and Lola were essentially second-generation WSC cars built to the newer Le Mans, regulations allowing them to carry bigger, more powerful engines and underside aerodynamics with rear diffusers in place of flat bottoms. The BMW had distinctive single roll-bar hoops for less drag.

The combination of the old and the new resulted in an entry of thirty prototypes at Sebring. After twelve hours, the winning BMW Motorsports entry led Dyson Racing's R&S MK III by just 9.207 seconds, the closest finish in the event's history. Both the entry list and the close finish encouraged the prospect of the older cars being able to compete with the new.

(From left) Butch Leitzinger, Elliott Forbes-Robinson, Rob Dyson, and Andy Wallace celebrate in Victory Lane.
*Rick Dole*

Fredy Lienhard and Didier Theys won the USRRC race at Lime Rock. They continued as teammates into the 2000s. *Rick Dole*

An immediate threat to the established WSC cars, the R8R was the first LMP1 prototype from Audi. The R8 came a year later. *Rick Dole*

A new arrival to sports car racing, ex-Formula One driver J. J. Lehto co-drove the BMW with Tom Kristensen, who scored the first of many major endurance victories, and Jörg Müller. Because Lehto did not enter under an IMSA license, he was not awarded points, which would have repercussions in the championship. Forbes-Robinson, Weaver, and Leitzinger were the runners-up, which also would have a bearing on the championship.

To keep the competition even, the ACO's intention was to use Balance of Performance (BOP) adjustments by employing engine restrictors to equate the two types of not-quite-identical basic prototype platforms. Based on horsepower and performance, the new BOP gave some consideration to aerodynamic adjustments as well, but no plan—such as wind tunnel testing—was in place to technically achieve this. Many consider this the year when the term BOP was first used. From the start, it was a questionable practice and became one of the biggest thorns in racers' minds in the decades that followed.

The second generation of cars with 6.0-liter displacement normally aspirated engines, such as the BMW LMR V12 and Panoz LMP-1, overshadowed the preexisting prototype participants, much to their chagrin. A team had to have 6.0 liters of displacement or a full-blown racing engine (4.0-liter Judd V10) to win. Stock block production-based 4.0- and 5.0-liter engines were no longer capable of winning. The chassis they were fitted to were not as aerodynamically developed, either.

Given the factory budgets, competitors with older WSC and IMSA GT cars gradually realized the gap was simply too big in both performance and the financial demands necessary to stay on a level playing field.

Several teams fielding the Ferrari 333SP, R&S MK III, and others continued in ALMS. By the second half of the year, the demise of the USRRC meant it was the only place left to race.

The Audi R8R and BMW V12 were rolled out at Sebring. The World Sports Cars led to the LMP1 class at Le Mans, which became a fixture in the ALMS. *Lee Self*

The unique front-mounted engine configuration of the road-going Panoz Esperante worked in both the LMP1 and GTR-1 versions. *Lee Self*

The Audis faltered at Sebring, in part because the front-mounted radiators generated too much heat, but they finished the grueling event. *Rick Dole*

The factory-backed Dodge Vipers and their V10 engines interrupted the contretemps between Porsche and Panoz in GTS-1. *Rick Dole*

The Road Atlanta race in the spring drew a deep field of cars, many of them familiar to fans and some new to IMSA.
*Rick Dole*

## VIPERS ARRIVE IN GT

The class structure enabled GT-1 cars to continue to race for overall race honors. In the absence of the Panoz GTR-1, which had been converted into the Panoz LMP-1, this left only the new Porsche GT-1 Evo to race against the prototypes, an indication that the concept of equating prototypes and the GT classes was not gaining much traction with factories or competitors.

The subcategories for GT cars in the ACO/Le Mans regulations resulted in factory-backed ORECA Dodge Viper GTS-R entries, a solo Saleen SR Ford, and numerous customer Porsche 911 Turbos. In the ALMS, these entries were designated GTS. The ever-popular, normally aspirated GT class attracted mostly Porsche 911 RSR and BMW M3 entries. A new Corvette program, meanwhile, was on the horizon.

Throughout the season, Panoz Motor Sports traded victories with the BMW Motorsport entry run by Schnitzer Motorsport and Charly Lamm. The BMW won four races and Panoz won three. Following its Sebring victory, the factory-backed BMW team did not show up at Road Atlanta for the second round. That left the door open, for the last time, to the original generation of WSC-type cars to have a shot at winning. Mimmo Schiattarella and van de Poele took advantage of the opportunity. They benefitted from the reworked aerodynamics of Team Rafanelli's R&S MK IIIs as well as their built-for-racing Judd V10 engine.

At Mosport in the third round, the BMWs were withdrawn over controversy about the safety of the circuit when the team's lead driver, Joachim Winkelhock, took exception to the track's safety. This was mostly due to the circumstance surrounding his older brother Manfred's fatal accident in a Porsche 962C at Turn Two during an FIA Group C World Championship race in 1985. The absence of the BMW left the door open for Jan Magnussen and Johnny O'Connell to take their lone victory of the season in the Panoz LMP-1.

Eric van de Poele and Mimmo Schiattarella scored the last IMSA win of the older generation WSC chassis onboard the Riley-Judd of Team Rafanelli. *Rick Dole*

The BMW V12 LMR won four of the eight races in the first year of the ALMS. *Rick Dole*

At Sonoma, Lehto and Steve Soper were back on top at the finish followed by two victories by the Panoz duo of Brabham and Bernard at Portland and Road Atlanta. Their second straight win came at the expense of Lehto and Jörg Mueller. The latter slid into the gravel at Turn Ten in the closing minutes of the Petit Le Mans despite a comfortable lead—this would be another key factor in the championship. Lehto and Soper won the final two events at Laguna Seca and Las Vegas, but it was Dyson's Forbes-Robinson who clinched the driver's championship despite not winning a race.

The ORECA Dodge Vipers won six straight races starting at Mosport as Olivier Beretta claimed the GTS driver's championship over frequent co-driver Karl Wendlinger. Following two Porsche victories to open the season, it was all Dodge and its V10 Viper. Co-driving with Patrick Huisman, Melanie and Martin Snow became the first husband and wife duo to win at Sebring in their 911 Turbo.

Milner's Prototype Technology Group and its M3 entries brought BMW the GT3 manufacturer championship after three victories and steady top five finishes. But the five victories of Cort Wagner on board the Alex Job Racing Porsche 911 RSR, including Sebring, clinched the driver's title.

The ever-growing number of the BMW entries from PTG dueled with the Porsches. *Rick Dole*

The Panoz LMP-1 Roadster S took its first win at Mosport and then captured two more to win the manufacturer championship. *Rick Dole*

The combination of the LMP1 class with WSC cars created a deep and colorful field heading into Turn One at Laguna Seca. *Rick Dole*

By the round at Portland in August, the LMP1 class prototypes were clearly demonstrating their aerodynamic and engine advantages. *Rick Dole*

## THE SALE TO PANOZ

From Mike Gue

"In late summer of 1999, we had a meeting of the four original PSR Holdings owners. It was looking more like a sale to Panoz would take place. Tom Milner and Doug Robinson also invited to our board meeting a representative of Panoz, which was totally unexpected for Ray and me. I thought, 'What's he doing here?' Milner informed us that he and Robinson had transferred their PSR Holdings stock to Panoz. That's how we found out that Panoz was now an equal partner.

"I told Tom and Doug that Ray and I would decide what we were going to do. I had kept in close contact with FIA President Max Mosley, because he was very worried about Don and the path he was taking. Max told us that as the president of PSR/IMSA only my signature would be accepted for the international listings for all the ALMS events in the US and Canada.

"This would be our trump card with Panoz. PSR was the sitting member in good standing on the competition board of ACCUS and had the corresponding sporting authority. Therefore, PSR was essential to the proper international listing of the ALMS events. ALMS had no sporting power whatsoever and would not be admitted to ACCUS until PSR altered its position with a sale.

"Panoz now controlled fifty percent of PSR's stock; the Sebring, Road Atlanta, and Mosport Park tracks; and a car company producing the Panoz LMP-1 prototype and GT-1 cars. He had almost all the pieces necessary to get the ALMS Series moving forward. So, we raised the issue, gently, about the position of the FIA and Mosley. But I told Ray privately, 'It's our trump card.'

"ALMS needed PSR/IMSA. But Panoz wanted total control of everything. Ray and I had to resign if the series was going to succeed. Negotiations were difficult, as Panoz wanted us to hand over our stock in the same terms that Doug and Milner had done. We intended to get what we felt we deserved for the balance of PSR Holdings stock we controlled. We weren't going to let it become a threat but would leverage our position with the FIA if needed.

"The negotiations came right up to the Petit Le Mans in 1999, because Panoz wanted to make the announcement of taking full control of the race along with the ACO. During negotiations with Don and his people, they would always change the contracts. There were a lot of red lines. With Ray's expertise, and after a lot of back and forth, we eventually arrived with an agreement that was acceptable.

"It got down to one point. Panoz wanted me to agree that I would never have any future involvement in the motorsport industry. Once Panoz finally dropped that requirement, we finalized the sale. We compromised a bit, because I was tired of all the fighting with Panoz. If we didn't get something done, all the work we had done rebuilding and trying to save the organization over the previous two years would have come to nothing."

# EPILOGUE

By September, PSR Holdings paid off the final note to Evans for the acquisition of the sanctioning body that had begun two years earlier, and they owned the company outright. By this time, the relationship between Panoz and the management at PSR Holdings had begun to sour. PSR and Gue continued to adeptly manage the ALMS races, but owner Panoz was becoming increasingly insistent about adding his input whether desired or not. Friction was developing about the disparity between how the ACO conducted its races at Le Mans and how PSR continued to conduct the ALMS races—which was according to its past IMSA procedures.

As the season ended, some teams had run for two years in two series using the same cars but to different specifications, all with mixed results. The ACO spec LMP-1s were clearly the cars to have in ALMS, but unfortunately none of the established US-based teams had access to such cars. Modifying their existing WSC chassis to the LMP specification was simply not practical, since the existing WSC cars were designed to maximize the original flat-bottom regulations, not the new ACO version of them. Changing it all was an entire redesign and too costly to contemplate when looking at the development gap necessary to catch up to the factory teams in LMP-1.

In October, the ALMS failed to pay the final event sanction fee to PSR Holdings for the season finale in Las Vegas. In November, Ray Smith began meetings with Don Panoz, initially in Las Vegas, focused on Panoz acquiring PSR and the IMSA brand. Once this lengthy discussion and transaction was completed in December 1999, Panoz owned the sanctioning body and the name IMSA with its value as the recognized sanctioning body for professional sports car endurance racing in the US.

Under trying circumstances, the core of IMSA and its legacy still existed due to the efforts of Gue and Smith. These two along with Tony Dowe, who became the technical director at the outset of the 1999 season, all departed PSR after the sale. The tumultuous decade of the 1990s ended with two different organizations, the ALMS and USRRC, running two different series. A new sanctioning body was on the horizon in the form of the Grand American Road Racing Association (Grand-Am) founded in mid-summer 1999 by the France family and associates.

The operational and marketing aspects of the USRRC management had not met the expectations of the primary stakeholders in Daytona Beach. USRRC sanctioned the 1999 Rolex 24 at Daytona and two other races before folding. The Daytona group saw limited potential in an IMSA series based on ACO rules and opted instead for a long-term approach based on cost-effective rules.

In 2000, the Grand-Am made its debut at the Rolex 24 at Daytona. The organization would take full advantage of the preexisting WSC and GT type cars that were being pushed away from the ALMS.

Once the ALMS and Grand-Am were firmly in place, the ensuing decade sustained this split before reunification occurred in 2012 when Panoz sold Road Atlanta, the lease to conduct races at Sebring, and the IMSA name to NASCAR Holdings.

Under the direction of Jim France, this long-sought reunification brought American professional sports car endurance racing back under one roof, starting in 2014. The occasion also marked the return of the original sanctioning body name of IMSA to prominence, but it was more than a branding exercise. Under the steady leadership of CEO Ed Bennett and President Scott Atherton, who was the long-serving president of the American Le Mans Series, the unified structure gave manufacturers and competitors confidence about the future.

A business model created by IMSA founder Bishop was essentially reestablished. It took into account the interests of all US participants, including track promoters, manufacturers, competitors, fans, and sponsors. IMSA's leadership soon began to look to the horizon, starting with the new Daytona Prototype International, or DPi, class. In GT, the popular Le Mans–based category for factory entrants used by the ALMS and the long-running GT Daytona (GTD) class of the Grand-Am, more focused on production specifications, were sustained.

The DPi class became the forerunner of a new Grand Touring Prototype (GTP) Series for hybrid prototypes with cost containment realized by using a common platform and approved builders. This bold new direction, under the leadership of President John Doonan, was pursued in conjunction with Le Mans officials, creating an unprecedented convergence of rules for the new hybrid prototypes. Known as Le Mans Daytona hybrid (LMDh) under the common platform used at IMSA and known as Hypercars under Le Mans rules—which allowed manufacturers to purpose-build their own cars—the convergence took to the track in 2023. The IMSA GT class transitioned, meanwhile, to the universal GT3 regulations for all participants in the GTD Pro and GTD ranks.

The result of the GTP and GT3 regulations were record IMSA crowds and a record number of participating manufacturers in the WeatherTech Sports Car Championship. True to the original vision of IMSA, the support series remained a high priority, also enjoying unprecedented success.

Two decades prior to this boom in professional sports car endurance racing, during the 1990s IMSA underwent its most chaotic and trying times. Enduring five different owners and four sales of the sanctioning body during these occasionally tumultuous years, IMSA maintained a competitive major league series that featured internationally recognized endurance racing events and a full schedule of races with robust starting fields of cars and world-class drivers. A long roster of supporting series and international forays by IMSA were also reminders of the strength of founder John Bishop's philosophy of how to bring professional road racing to North America. Following Bishop's departure, a dedicated staff helped ensure the original vision for IMSA was sustained, preserving the long-term opportunity for sports car endurance racing to continue thriving.

# ACKNOWLEDGMENTS

Trying to capture the tumultuous nature of IMSA and sports car racing over the 1990s was a challenge.

Special acknowledgment and thanks go to my coauthors for contributing their personal experience and insight—former IMSA President George Silbermann, longtime crewman Martin Raffauf, and veteran journalist Jonathan Ingram. A special thanks to Jonathan for his meticulous editing skills while bringing a lot of different elements into a readable book!

In addition, special acknowledgment and thanks go to the six key individuals who were willing to share how a decade in IMSA impacted their teams, their business, and their personal lives.

Rob Dyson, Wayne Taylor, and Fredy Lienhard contributed stories as team owners and drivers. Bill Riley of Riley Technologies and Luca Pignacca of Dallara Automobiles and Ferrari provided insights about the two most significant race cars of the decade. Along with Ray Smith, contributor Michael Gue had a unique role of guiding the sport through its most difficult times.

Using images as well as words, we wanted to rekindle the sensory experience of motor racing's sights, sounds, and smells from a bygone era. Special thanks go to everyone who submitted images, especially those whose photos are included: Bruce Clarke, Brian Cleary, Rick Dole, Tony Dowe, Peter Gloede, Brian Doc Mitchell, Mark Raffauf, Lee Self, and Bill Tuttle.

Most of the images are pre-digital color slides or black-and-white negatives. In some cases, they were dug out of files and basements after many years of lying low in the dark. Thanks to those who did the digging to help shed light on IMSA history.

The visual presentation would not have been complete without access to the IMSA Archive, the Costos Los Collection, the NASCAR Archive and Research Center, and the Porsche AG Archive.

Trying to give all participants their due justice visually was just not possible. We hope the written description of what was occurring on the racetrack will bring back memories for those who were there and helped create the great competition.

A big thank you to the team led by publisher Lee Klancher at Octane Press, where production editor Faith Garcia kept us all organized.

Most importantly, thanks to the thousands of fans and TV viewers who continued to come out to watch the racers and their cars. By this decade of IMSA a second generation of fans who initially were brought to the races by their families were bringing their own children. By the end of the 1990s, a new century of "Racing with a Difference" and "World Class Competition" beckoned!

—Mark Raffauf

# INDEX

*"He looked like a crook, acted like a crook, and in fact was a crook"*

**Mark Raffauf**

*"When I returned to the office after my meeting with new IMSA owner Charlie Slater I got out of the car in the parking lot. A horn honked. It was Mike Cone. Cone rolled down the window of his SUV, briefly thanked me for the hard work over the years, said he was sorry, rolled the window back up, then drove away."*

**George Silbermann**

*"I loved the racing format and all I knew about was IMSA. I got to know everyone in IMSA and found it to be a very professional organization from the facts of understanding technology, whether it be chassis or engine or anything. They gave us a platform to do what we wanted to do."*

**Wayne Taylor**

*"Not a day goes by that I am not thankful for the opportunities we have had and for what we accomplished. What a privilege it was to witness and experience this incredible era of racing."*

**Rob Dyson**